Mackinac

An Island Famous in These Regions

Mackinac State Historic Parks
Mackinac Island, Michigan
©1998 Mackinac State Historic Parks

ISBN 911872-68-X soft cover
ISBN 911872-69-9 hard cover

First Edition

First Printing   5,000 copies, soft cover
                 2,000 copies, hard cover

Third Printing 3,000 copies, soft cover

Text: Phil Porter
Art Direction: Thomas Kachadurian

Contents

MACKINAC:
An Island Famous in These Regions

MACKINAC ISLAND HAS ALWAYS been a special place. More than 300 years ago the Jesuit missionary Father Claude Dablon, after listening to Native American stories and legends, described Mackinac as "an island famous in these regions." Mackinac is still famous today, even though the waves of history have washed new peoples, industries, and technology onto her shores. These changes have enhanced, not reduced, Mackinac Island's distinctive character and allure.

What is it that makes Mackinac Island such a special place? Certainly geography is part of the story. For centuries the Great Lakes served as a water highway connecting distant peoples and places. Mackinac Island, in the center of this water highway, became a logical and convenient gathering place for water travelers. These same waters gave life to abundant natural resources, which provided food for subsistence and products for Mackinac's earliest industries. The surrounding lakes also contribute to the island's natural beauty, another component of its enchantment. Location, natural resources, and beauty have combined to make Mackinac Island a renowned summer gathering place for centuries.

This is the story of Mackinac Island as seen through the experiences of the people who gathered here: worshipers, hunters, traders, soldiers, fishermen, and tourists. No single group of gatherers, no single chapter in Mackinac Island's history, takes precedence. It is the sum of its many chapters that makes Mackinac such an interesting, important, and, yes, famous place.

"Missilimakinac is an island famous in these regions… It is situated exactly in the strait connecting the Lake of the Hurons and that of the Illinois, and forms the key and the door, so to speak, for all the peoples of the south, as does the Sault of the North; for in these regions there are only those two passages by water for very many Nations, who must seek one or the other of the two if they wish to visit the French settlements."
Father Claude Dablon 1670

Natamissing Bemadisidjig Mishinimakinang *(The First People of Michilimackinac)*

GREAT LAKES NATIVE AMERICANS were Mackinac Island's first summer visitors. These Woodland-period (1,000 B.C. to 1650 A.D.), semi-nomadic people traveled the Great Lakes by season in search of food. In the winter, small family groups camped near the wild game habitats, hunting and trapping deer, elk, moose, bear, beaver, and muskrat. Springtime found them traveling to maple forests where they tapped trees, gathered sap, and boiled it down to sugar. In canoes loaded with dried meat and mokuks (small birch bark containers) of sugar, Native families paddled to the Straits of Mackinac in early summer, where they gathered in large villages to fish for trout, pike, sturgeon, herring, and whitefish. So plentiful were the fish at Mackinac that the Native people called these waters "the home of the fish." Archaeologists have unearthed prehistoric Native American summer fishing camps at St. Ignace, Bois Blanc Island, Mackinaw City, and Mackinac Island. Bone fishhooks, clay pottery sherds,

Sa-wa-ne-me-ka struggled as he hoisted his fish-filled net out of the water. The glimmering trout and whitefish filled the bottom of his canoe as he paddled back to the island village. For many generations Sa-wa-ne-me-ka's family traveled to this sacred island every summer to fish the nearby waters. As the bronze-skinned fisherman guided his canoe back to shore, he saw, in the island's hump-backed landscape, the image of the turtle's back rising from the water. Once again Sa-wa-ne-me-ka realized why his people had named this place Michilimackinac, Land of the Great Turtle.

and stone spear heads reveal the activities that took place at least 700 years before Europeans arrived in the Straits of Mackinac.

Although Native people camped throughout the straits region, they considered Mackinac Island, with its towering bluffs and dramatic limestone formations, a special and sacred place. According to ancient Native tradition, Mackinac Island was the first land to appear after the waters of the Great Flood began to recede. The Great Hare, Michibou, retrieved a grain of sand from the lake bed beneath the waters and blew on it until it expanded into an island. The first man was put on the island and from here his descendants spread to the rest of the earth. Even today, Native people from

ABOVE: **For centuries, Native Americans had summer fishing villages on Mackinac Island and throughout the straits region.** LEFT: **This clay bowl sherd excavated at Colonial Michili-mackinac, bears testimony to pre-historic Native American settlement at the straits.**

Chippewa mode of traveling in the winter.

throughout the Great Lakes region continue to revere Mackinac Island as a place of great spiritual importance.

The history and oral traditions of Mackinac's first settlers are kept alive by the Ojibway (Chippewa) and Odawa (Ottawa) people who still live in the region. These tribes, along with the Potawatomi, are the Anishnabeg people who migrated to the Great Lakes from the Atlantic coast during the Woodland period. According to Ojibway legend, the three tribes separated at the Straits of Mackinac. When the first Europeans came to the Straits of Mackinac in the 1670s, it was the Anishnabeg people who welcomed and shared with them the ancient traditions of the Land of the Great Turtle.

French soldiers at Fort DuBuade in St. Ignace regulated and protected the French fur trade in the 1690s.

Early European Settlement

DRAWN BY THE STRAITS of Mackinac's central location and rich supply of fish, Jesuit priests and French fur traders established villages here in the late seventeenth century. In 1670 Father Claude Dablon journeyed from his Ojibway mission at Sault Ste. Marie to study the possibility of establishing a mission on Mackinac Island. Impressed by what he found, Dablon encouraged Father Jacques Marquette to bring his refugee band of Huron to Mackinac. Marquette's band of displaced Huron had been seeking a home ever since they were driven out of southern Ontario by Iroquois warriors in the 1650s. Pushed to the western shore of Lake Superior, the Huron briefly settled at Marquette's mission of Saint-Esprit at La Pointe (today Madeline Island, Wisconsin) in Sioux territory. When conflict erupted between the Huron and the Sioux, Marquette eagerly moved his faithful congregation to the safety of Mackinac Island in the spring of 1671. The agricultural Huron found the thin soils of Mackinac Island unsuitable for their crops.

Within the year, Marquette and the Huron moved to the more fertile land on the north shore of the straits. Here Marquette established the permanent mission of St. Ignatius Loyola (today St. Ignace, Michigan), named in honor of the founder of the Jesuit order. Nearby the Jesuits also established the Mission of St. Francis Borgia to serve the Odawa, another agricultural tribe

"In the neighborhood of this island, as being the spot most noted in all these regions for its abundance of fish, various Peoples used to make their abode, who now fully intend to return thither if they see the peace is firmly established. It is for this reason that we have already begun to found the Mission of St. Ignatius; this being done during the past winter, which we spent there."
Father Claude Dablon 1671

Traders, who gathered the furs from Native Americans in the wilderness, brought their pelts to the Straits of Mackinac in early summer.

Also in early summer, merchants shipped 90-pound bales of trade goods in large 40-foot long canoes from eastern cities to the Straits of Mackinac.

While at the Straits, traders received a fresh supply of goods for another winter of trading and merchants loaded furs into their canoes for the journey back to the east.

living on the St. Ignace peninsula.

While Jesuit missionaries endeavored to convert the Native people to Christianity, French entrepreneurs looked to do business with them. The central location of the Straits of Mackinac on the water highway system and the proximity of numerous Native tribes made it an ideal home base for the French upper Great Lakes fur trade. The 1670s fur trade community at St. Ignace established a seasonal industry that continued at the Straits of Mackinac for the next 150 years. Every summer, freight canoes arrived at St. Ignace from Montreal with tons of European-manufactured goods. Traders bundled up an assortment of items and left the straits in smaller canoes bound for winter camps along the rivers and streams of the Great Lakes watershed. After a winter of exchanging blankets, beads, kettles, and guns for Indian-trapped beaver, muskrat, otter, and fox pelts, traders returned to St. Ignace, where they warehoused the furs until they could ship them to Montreal. Meanwhile, the traders outfitted themselves with another winter's supply of merchandise. Thus the Straits of Mackinac functioned as a fur trade summer depot and trans-shipment center through the French and British periods and for nearly half a century of American settlement.

Within a decade, soldiers arrived at the straits and established a pattern of military activity that continued for more than two hundred years. In representing their government's interests, soldiers constructed forts, developed and maintained alliances with Native

Americans, organized and executed military raids, and regulated and protected commercial interests. French soldiers built the area's first fort at St. Ignace in the 1680s. The military commanders of Fort DuBuade, supported by French Marines, checked traders' licenses, protected the St. Ignace community, and recruited Native warriors to block English expansion into the western Great Lakes.

A glut of furs in European markets convinced the French government to abandon Fort DuBuade in 1697. To stop the flow of pelts out of North America, the French Crown revoked trade licenses and closed military posts. Despite the official retreat, a thriving settlement, including the Jesuit missions and unlicensed traders, or Coureurs de Bois, remained at St. Ignace. Four years later the French soldiers returned to the Great Lakes and built a new fort at Detroit. The fort's charismatic new commander, Antoine de la Mothe Cadillac, convinced several bands of western Great Lakes Indians, including the St. Ignace Huron, to move near his new post. This band of Huron later became known as Wyandots. The Odawa chose to stay at St. Ignace. Sometime before 1714, the Odawa and Jesuit missionaries, having exhausted their

OPPOSITE: **This serpentine side plate is from a flintlock musket, a common 18th-century trade item.** ABOVE: **Modern-day interpreters reenact the backbreaking work of 18th-century voyageurs.** BELOW: **During the 18th and 19th centuries millions of beaver pelts were shipped through Mackinac to Europe for manufacturing hats.**

An Island Famous in These Regions   **9**

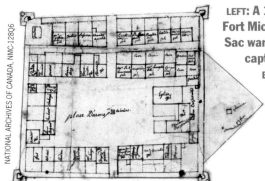

LEFT: A 1749 plan of Fort Michilimackinac RIGHT: Fort Michilimackinac's Land Gate. Ojibway and Sac warriors raced through this gate when they captured the fort in June 1763.
BELOW: Mackinac Island's Skull Cave, hiding place for Alexander Henry.

fields at St. Ignace, moved to fresh soil on the south shore of the Straits of Mackinac (today, Mackinaw City). When French soldiers returned in 1714 they followed the Odawa and Jesuits and built Fort Michilimackinac.

Throughout the eighteenth century Michilimackinac grew and prospered as a strategic military post and principal summer depot for the upper Great Lakes fur trade. The village was geographically well situated for gathering troops to support French military objectives. French commanders led war parties comprised of European soldiers and Native warriors from Michilimackinac during the Fox and the French and Indian wars. While soldiers flexed their military might, fur traders expanded the village. Carpenters built new rowhouses in the 1730s, erected Ste. Anne's Church in 1743, and added a new guardhouse in 1751. French fur traders and soldiers married Odawa and Ojibway women and their mixed-blood, or Métis, children became the dominant population of the Straits of Mackinac region until the 1820s.

British soldiers and government officials peacefully took command of Fort Michilimackinac in 1761 as a result of their conquest of Canada during the Seven Years' War. British fur traders, including Alexander Henry, accompanied the soldiers and established their businesses at Michilimackinac.

While French inhabitants generally welcomed the British, Native people remained wary. Odawa, Ojibway and other Indians fought side-by-side with the French during the war and, although the French had surrendered, the Native people insisted that they had not been conquered. Arrogant British policies that ignored established trade and gift-giving patterns

further irritated the Indians. These tensions erupted into a bloody conflict in 1763 when Ojibway and Sac warriors attacked Michilimackinac as part of a broader Indian stroke against British posts in North America known as Pontiac's Rebellion. The warriors executed a swift and deadly attack that left twenty one British soldiers dead at Michilimackinac. The surviving soldiers, along with English traders, were held captive except for Alexander Henry who managed to escape with the help of his friend Minavavana. The Ojibway chief quietly took Henry to Mackinac Island and hid him in an ancient cave filled with human bones now known as Skull Cave.

British troops returned to Michilimackinac in 1764 and adjusted their policies to meet Indian approval. Once peace was restored the fur trade prospered under British rule and the community expanded. Builders enlarged the fort to accommodate new construction; by the 1770s, "suburbs" of more than one hundred houses lined the beach east of the fort.

Over time British commanders developed strong alliances with the region's Native Americans. These efforts proved valuable during the American Revolution when Odawa, Ojibway, Winnebago, Sac, Fox, Menominee, and Sioux warriors joined British soldiers from Michilimackinac to fight American rebels at Montreal, New York, and Kentucky.

While British officers led raids from Michilimackinac, American troops under the command of Colonel George Rogers Clark captured British posts in Indiana and Illinois, and jeopardized the security of Michilimackinac. Clark's soldiers, aided by pro-American French inhabitants, seized Vincennes, Kaskaskia, and Cahokia in 1778 and threatened to sail against Fort Michilimackinac from southern Lake Michigan. This threat, as well as growing unrest among the neighboring Odawa and Ojibway, convinced British authorities to find a more defensible location in the Straits of Mackinac. The towering bluffs of Mackinac Island - the turtle's back - provided the ideal situation for the new fort.

An Island Famous in These Regions   **11**

The Revolution at Mackinac

WHILE SAILING TO HIS NEW COMMAND at Fort Michilimackinac in October 1779, Patrick Sinclair took a brief detour to survey Mackinac Island. Convinced that the shore-hugging, wooden-palisaded post of Michilimackinac could not withstand an American attack, the British commander anxiously sought a more defensible location. A quick tour of Mackinac Island convinced him that the island's imposing limestone bluffs and deep harbor provided the necessary protection. Sinclair immediately began to design a new fortification and plan his move. Before the transfer could begin, however, Sinclair had to secure permission from the resident Ojibway.

Although Europeans had not lived on Mackinac Island since Marquette's brief stay more than 100 years earlier, the island had not been unoccupied. Ojibway families returned each summer to fish in the straits and plant a little corn in the island's rocky soil. Birch bark wigwams ringed the crescent bay on the island's southern shore beneath the bluff that Sinclair longingly eyed for his new fort. Sinclair began negotiations by sending the Métis alliance chief, Charles Gauthier, to the island's Ojibway chief with a string of wampum and an explanation of Sinclair's plan. Gauthier secured per-

"On my way to this place I stop't at Michilimackinac Island for several hours…The situation is respectable and convenient for a Fort…"

Lieutenant Governor Patrick Sinclair 1779

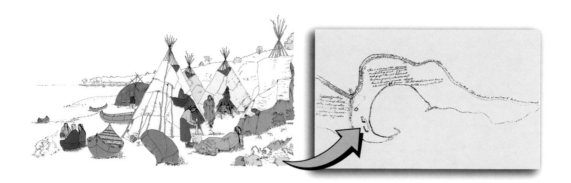

mission, and Sinclair immediately sent a detachment of soldiers to begin clearing brush.

The final transfer of Mackinac Island was completed in a formal ceremony that took place in a maple grove below the fort on May 12, 1781. The Ojibway chiefs Kitchie Negon, Pouanas, Koupe, and Magousseihigan agreed to sell the island to Great Britain for a dozen canoes loaded with goods and merchandise valued at £5,000. Sinclair drafted a formal deed which was witnessed and signed by representatives of both the military and civilian communities. The Ojibway leaders validated the document with their totem marks in the left margin. Kitchie Negon and the other Ojibway had little use for the English deed and preferred to memorialize the sale with a wampum belt. To this end, Sinclair presented them with a seven-foot belt which was to be kept in the Ojibway village as a "lasting memorial" of the transaction.

The move to Mackinac Island provided Sinclair with an opportunity to restructure the relationship between the military and the community. Michilimackinac's commanders had long realized the inherent security problem of having soldiers and civilians living within the same protective walls. Sinclair eliminated this problem by separating the two, putting soldiers in a fort on the bluff and civilians in a village below. Sensing that mainland inhabitants might be reluctant to move to the island, Sinclair ordered Ste. Anne's Church dismantled and shipped over the ice

OPPOSITE TOP: **The deed to Mackinac Island. This document confirmed the sale of Mackinac Island by the Ojibway to the British government.** OPPOSITE BOTTOM: **Silhouette of Patrick Sinclair.** ABOVE: **Patrick Sinclair's 1779 sketch (right) of Mackinac Island harbor showing "Indian Huts" near the shore.**

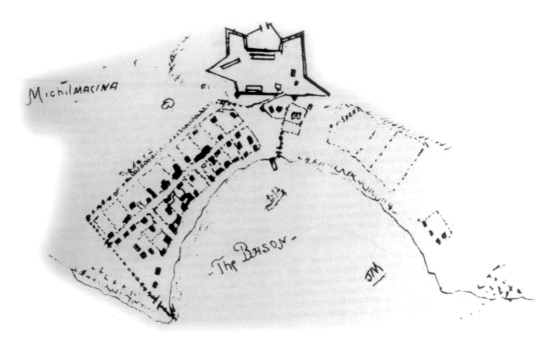

by ox-drawn sleds to the new village in February 1780. Sinclair correctly assumed that the predominantly Roman Catholic population would eagerly follow their beloved church. In order to provide some level of protection for the community, Sinclair built a wooden palisade wall on the east, north, and west sides of the village. The bay bordered the village on the south. Inside the protective walls, the people constructed houses along two parallel streets (today's Main and Market streets) which were connected by narrow alleys (Fort, Astor, and Hoban streets, and French Lane). Several of these eighteenth-century log homes still stand in the island's village today, disguised beneath modern exteriors. The north fence line, once the site of an imposing picket wall, is now marked by a modern cyclone fence along the eighth fairway of Grand Hotel's Jewel golf course.

From the beginning, British military engineers realized that Fort Mackinac was dominated by a high bluff in the center of the island. Enemy cannon placed at this strategic spot could easily bombard the fort. Although the south edge of this upper bluff would have been the safest, most defensible location for the fort, Sinclair judged that it was too far from the harbor and village. In the end Sinclair's choice was a compromise that allowed him to protect the village and dominate the harbor to the south, while leaving him vulnerable to attack from the north. Ironically, British soldiers used Sinclair's compromise to their advantage twenty years later when they attacked the American-held fort at the outbreak of the War of 1812.

Construction of Fort Mackinac progressed slowly and at great expense. Soldiers successfully moved and reconstructed several buildings, including the soldiers' barracks, guardhouse, and provision storehouse. New construction included the stone walls, bastions, and powder magazine. Sinclair also began (but never finished) the Officers' Stone Quarters, a 100-foot-long structure that would serve both as a blockhouse and barracks. The fort was only partially completed when Sinclair razed and burned the remains of Fort Michilimackinac and moved his men to the island in the summer of 1781. By the end of the summer Sinclair had already spent more than £41,000 on his unfinished fort. In addition to his heavy construction expenses, Sinclair had run up huge debts in the Indian Department, especially in distributing gifts. An audit of his expenditures resulted in charges of financial mismanagement; Sinclair was forced to relinquish his command in order to defend himself to authorities in Quebec.

An Island Famous in These Regions   **15**

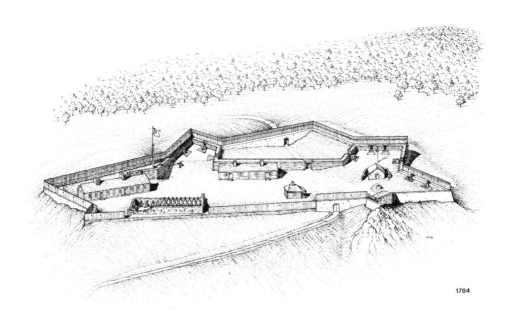

1784

ABOVE: **Fort Mackinac, as it was originally designed and constructed by Patrick Sinclair in the early 1780s.** RIGHT: **The Officers Stone Quarters remained unfinished until American soldiers completed the task in 1800.**

Captain Daniel Robertson replaced Sinclair in 1782. Despite the American victory at Yorktown, Virginia, Robertson continued to work on the fort while negotiators settled the countries' differences. In May 1783 Robertson abruptly halted all construction when he received the unwelcome details of the Paris peace treaty. The joy that accompanied the announcement of peace was tempered by provisions in the treaty that established a new Great Lakes border between British Canada and the United States. Angered and frustrated, Robertson realized that the treaty put Mackinac Island in the United States.

America Comes To Mackinac

SEVERAL IMPORTANT BRITISH FORTS became United States property following the Revolution. The loss of these strategic posts - Fort Oswego and Fort Niagara on Lake Ontario, Fort Miamis in Ohio (on the Maumee River) and the forts at Detroit and Mackinac Island - threatened British control of the upper Great Lakes fur trade and alliances with powerful Indian nations. Political pressure from English merchants prompted Great Britain to hold on to these important posts for thirteen years after the peace treaty was signed. The United States Army, lacking the soldiers needed to man these distant posts, was unable to force the British out.

Fort Mackinac deteriorated during this thirteen-year period. British authorities refused to appropriate funds for renovations or improvements to a fort that belonged to the United States. The walls crumbled, logs rotted, and the Officers' Stone Quarters remained an empty, unfinished shell. In their decaying post, British commanders continued the vital task of safeguarding the fur trade and preserving relationships with Native peoples.

While the fort languished, the civilian community flourished as British merchants continued to ply the fur trade. With little fear of attack, residents began building outside the original town walls. New homes

"The post now committed to your charge is of the first consequence, being Grand depot of merchandise for the outfits of the British traders ...add to this, that it is surrounded by the most numerous and powerful tribes of Indians in the wilderness of the west."
General Anthony Wayne to Fort Mackinac commander Major Henry Burbeck, 1796

An Island Famous in These Regions **17**

appeared on the east end of town and small farms began to dot the island's more fertile higher-elevation lands. Dr. David Mitchell established his 110-acre farm in the center of the island (today's Harrisonville) and George Schindler cultivated land along the island's southwest bluff.

Jay's Treaty, which sought to resolve lingering differences between the United States and Great Britain, paved the way for American soldiers to occupy Fort Mackinac on September 1, 1796. While waiting to surrender the fort, the British constructed a new post at St. Joseph's Island on the Canadian side of St. Mary's River, about forty miles east of Mackinac. Great Britain would continue to exert her influence in the Straits of Mackinac region from Fort St. Joseph.

American troops, under the command of Major Henry Burbeck, faced a daunting task in rebuilding Fort Mackinac. As Burbeck surveyed the post, he discovered the extensive deterioration caused by British neglect. The commander took immediate action to prepare the post for the coming winter, but delayed major construction until the following year. In August 1797, General James Wilkinson traveled to Mackinac to inspect the works and make the final decision on what to do with Fort

ERIC MANDERS

Mackinac. Like the British engineers before him, Wilkinson could not ignore the fort's fundamental defensive flaw: It was dominated by the island's high bluff, therefore unable to stop a major offensive assault from the north. No expense or design could overcome this defect, so Wilkinson focused on making the fort "impregnable to the attacks of small armys." Stone and heavy timber blockhouses, built on the old British bastions, provided defense along the fort's perimeter. New stone walls with nine-foot pickets replaced rotted wooden walls along the southern bluff; the massive stone ravelin became the north wall.

The extensive rebuilding project was completed in 1800 when American soldiers finished the Officers' Stone Quarters, a building begun eighteen years earlier by the British. The basic configuration established during this three-year project remained unchanged throughout the rest of the fort's history.

Northwest Territory secretary Winthrop Sargent accompanied Burbeck to Mackinac in order to establish United States civil authority. During the fall of 1796 Sargent examined land records, appointed justices of the peace, commissioned militia officers, and met with area Odawa and Ojibway. The island's civilian settlement had continued to grow during this early American period, as new houses were built and additional land was put under cultivation. Among the new farms were those owned by ex-Fort Mackinac soldier Ambrose Davenport (today's Hubbard Annex) and Simon Champaign (today's Stonecliffe and Woods Golf Course). Sargent incorporated Mackinac Island into Wayne County, which was then a vast tract of land that included most of Michigan, northern portions of Ohio and Indiana, and sections of Illinois and Wisconsin bordering on Lake Michigan. During his three-week

An Island Famous in These Regions   **19**

stay on Mackinac Island, Sargent successfully brought the upper Great Lakes under the jurisdiction of the United States government. The burden of enforcing federal authority and protecting commercial and military interests fell on the shoulders of Major Burbeck and his troops.

Provisions in Jay's Treaty made it difficult for American merchants to enter the fur trade at Mackinac in the late 1790s. The treaty allowed Canadians to move freely across the border and continue to trade in United States territory. With an established network of traders, outposts and centralized depots like the one at Mackinac, British companies maintained a firm grip on the fur trade. American merchants, including John Jacob Astor, bitterly complained about their inability to establish a fur trading foothold on United States soil. Most were reconciled to operating as middlemen, purchasing furs from Canadian firms and selling them to American and European markets.

In 1811 Astor's American Fur Company merged with the Montreal Michilimackinac Company. As a result of this partnership, Astor controlled part of the Great Lakes fur trade. An American merchant finally had a foothold in the lucrative Mackinac trade. But just as Astor was establishing his Mackinac empire, the United States and Great Britain went to war. Astor watched and worried while Mackinac Island and its prosperous fur trade became one of the battlegrounds of the War of 1812.

War at Mackinac, 1812-1815

WAR BROKE OUT between the United States and Great Britain in the summer of 1812. Relations between the two countries had been strained since the Revolution. In the Midwest, British-supplied Indians attacked American settlements in Indiana and Illinois. On the high seas the British navy harassed United States merchant ships and impressed American soldiers. In retaliation, the United States government banned British imports. Angered citizens pressured politicians to declare war. As antagonism escalated into conflict, Mackinac Island became a center of attention.

Rumors of war reached British troops at Fort St. Joseph in the spring of 1812. Here, British authorities gathered about 400 Odawa, Ojibway, Menominee, Winnebago, and Dakota warriors. These sympathetic Native Americans, along with 150 French-Canadian and Métis voyageurs and nearly fifty red-coated soldiers, constituted an imposing force ready to support the British cause. On July 8, British commander Captain Charles Roberts learned that war had been declared. Eight days later he sailed to attack Fort Mackinac.

The unusual movement of Native Americans through the Straits of Mackinac alarmed Lieutenant Porter Hanks, Fort Mackinac's twenty-four-year-old American commander. On July 16,

"Yesterday two Indians arrived here from Michilimackinac, who bring the unwelcome tidings of that post having fallen into the hands of the British. They say that before the news of war reached that place, a party of British and Indians…proceeded from Fort St. Joseph, where the news had been for days."
The New-England Palladium
August 18, 1812
Boston, Massachusetts

An Island Famous in These Regions   **21**

LEFT: 1813 engraving of Mackinac Island village, harbor and fort from Windermere Point. BELOW LEFT: British attack route, July 1812. BELOW RIGHT: Michael Dousman. OPPOSITE TOP: Fort Mackinac's west blockhouse with village and harbor below. OPPOSITE BOTTOM: Sergeant, British Royal Artillery, 1814-15.

Hanks sent Mackinac Militia Captain Michael Dousman by canoe to spy on the British at Fort St. Joseph. Dousman was only fifteen miles from Mackinac Island when attacking British troops captured him. Captain Roberts released Dousman, instructing him to warn and protect the village citizens. In return, Dousman agreed not to inform the American garrison of the impending British attack. Roberts landed his force on the north side of the island under cover of darkness. While Dousman moved civilians to safety, Roberts' voyageurs hauled two six-pound cannons to the high bluff behind Fort Mackinac, and the warriors and soldiers took positions in the woods behind the fort. True to his word, Dousman kept silent and the British moved into position without resistance. The next morning Roberts commenced his attack by firing a warning shot from one of the six-pounders. He sent a flag of truce and a summons to surrender to Lieutenant Hanks who, for the first time, learned that war had been declared. It was shortly after 10:00 a.m. on July 17, 1812. The war's first land action was underway.

Hanks had few options. He faced an overwhelming force of 600 hostile troops and two deadly cannons aimed at the most defenseless part of a fort that was only "impregnable to the attacks of small armys." This was no small army. With a force of less than sixty men, Hanks surrendered without a fight in order to "prevent a general massacre."

Captain Roberts took command of Fort Mackinac and confined Lieutenant Hanks and his soldiers until they could be sent on parole to the American post at Detroit. Most civilians remained on the island after they swore allegiance to King George III. Ambrose Davenport, John Dousman, and Samuel Abbott

refused to sign the British oath. In one of the great statements of American patriotism Davenport declared, "I was born in America, and am determined, at all hazards, to live and die an American citizen." Captain Roberts arrested all three and sent them to Detroit with the American soldiers. Davenport was forced to leave his wife Elizabeth and six children alone on their island farm.

The United States war effort on the Great Lakes dramatically improved in 1813. On September 10, Commander Oliver Hazard Perry's navy defeated Captain Robert Barclay's British fleet on Lake Erie. Perry's victory opened the way for United States troops to regain the upper Great Lakes. In anticipation of an American counterattack, British soldiers reinforced their defenses on Mackinac Island. By the summer of 1814 the fort's picket walls had been replaced; a contingent of volunteers, the "Michigan Fencibles," had been raised; additional regular troops had been assigned to the post; and construction of a new fortification had been completed. The new fort, named Fort George in honor of the king, was built on the island heights, thereby eliminating Fort Mackinac's chief defensive weakness. British efforts in strengthening their position were not in vain. The long-expected American expedition appeared off the island's southeast shore in late July 1814.

The American force consisted of the brigs *Niagara* and *Lawrence* and the schooners *Caledonia*, *Tigress*, and *Scorpion* under the command of Commodore Arthur Sinclair. On board, Lieutenant Colonel George Croghan commanded a force of more than 750 soldiers. To test the possibility of a frontal attack, sailors guided the *Lawrence* into the bay and fired their cannon at the fort's south wall. The gunners soon realized that they could not elevate their cannon high enough to hit the fort walls, and the *Lawrence* retreated as the British returned fire. It was now Croghan's turn, and he decided to copy the British strategy of

two years earlier: land on the north side of the island and attack the fort from behind.

To counter the American land attack, British commander Lieutenant Colonel Robert McDouall marched most of his soldiers from Fort Mackinac to a ridge above Michael Dousman's farm in the center of the island. British redcoats, supported by 350 Native American warriors of various nations, took a commanding position from which to ambush the United States force. British cannons pounded American infantrymen as they advanced across the open fields. McDouall sent Chief Tomah's Menominee warriors to protect his left flank against an American assault led by Major Andrew Hunter Holmes. During the battle more than a dozen United States soldiers, including Major Holmes, were killed and many more were wounded. Battered by the British force, the Americans retreated to their ships. Relieved and

Opposite top: Artists rendering of the Battle of Mackinac Island at Michael Dousman's farm, August 4, 1814. OPPOSITE BOTTOM: 1936 reconstruction of Fort Holmes. RIGHT: Fragment of a United States Corps of Artillery cap plate, worn by an American soldier at Fort Mackinac c.1815. BELOW: Josiah Jebb's painting of Odawa Indians from Mackinac Island, 1814.

jubilant that the British suffered only a few casualties, McDouall ordered his soldiers back to Fort Mackinac where the British Union Jack still flew in the breeze.

Where American soldiers failed on the battlefield, their negotiators succeeded at the peace table. On Christmas Eve 1814, the United States and Great Britain signed the Treaty of Ghent, ending the War of 1812. The treaty required both sides to return captured lands. At Mackinac, McDouall received the news with mixed emotions. Although pleased that the war was over, the British commander was furious about surrendering Fort Mackinac. After risking his life defending the island, successfully repelling the American attack, and investing time and energy into building Fort George, McDouall was ordered to retreat. Commenting on the treaty, McDouall bitterly complained, "Our negotiators, as usual, have been egregiously duped. I am penetrated by grief at the restoration

of this fine island - a Fortress built by nature for herself." On July 18, 1815, United States troops took command of Fort Mackinac and Fort George (later renamed Fort Holmes in honor of the fallen American major) and McDouall led the last British soldiers from Mackinac Island.

An Island Famous in These Regions   **25**

LEFT: 1821-pattern, bell-crowned leather cap. This was the dress cap of American soldiers stationed at Fort Mackinac from 1821-1832, during the height of the American fur trade. RIGHT: Mackinac Island with Round Island in the foreground, by F. S. Bolton, 1817. BELOW: Sergeant, United States Infantry, 1825.

The Flourishing Fur Trade

JOHN JACOB ASTOR reestablished the American Fur Company on Mackinac Island after the War of 1812. By the 1820s the fur trade was flourishing. Mackinac Island, connecting the fur-bearing regions of the upper Midwest with East Coast and European markets, became one of Astor's most valuable trading posts.

As a summer depot and supply station, Mackinac Island continued to function for Astor as it had for British and French fur merchants before him. The island's permanent population of about 500 French Canadians, Métis, and Americans swelled to more than 2,000 during the summer rendezvous. Traders returned to the island from western and northern Michigan, Wisconsin, Minnesota, Iowa, Illinois, and Indiana in canoes loaded with thousands of fur pelts. Native Americans from many nations arrived to buy supplies and conduct business with the United States Indian Agent. Company clerks traveled from New York and took their stations at tables and desks in the company warehouse on Market Street (today's Community Hall). Here, amidst the pungent odor of raw pelts and sweaty voyageurs, clerks worked long into the night counting, sorting, grading, and repacking beaver, muskrat, otter, marten, fox, mink, badger, raccoon, and other furs.

"These were the palmy days of Mackinac. As the headquarters of the American Fur Company, and the 'entrepot' of the whole Northwest, all the trade in supplies and goods on the one hand, and in furs and products of the Indian country on the other, was in the hands of the parent establishment or its numerous outposts scattered along Lakes Superior and Michigan, the Mississippi, or through still more distant regions."

Juliette Kinzie
Mackinac, 1830

An Island Famous in These Regions   **27**

Particularly popular were beaver pelts which were used to make hats beginning with seventeenth-century tri-corns and continuing to nineteenth-century top hats. The rebaled furs were shipped to company warehouses in New York City, where Astor strategically distributed them to merchants and hatters in England, Germany, China, France, and North America. The fashion industry transformed these North American furs into a variety of garments from mittens and muffs to hats and fur-trimmed cloaks.

Astor's Mackinac Island establishment was run by partner and general manager Ramsey Crooks, who divided his time between New York and Mackinac, and resident manager Robert Stuart. From his home next door to the warehouse (today's Stuart House), Stuart carefully oversaw the distribution of supplies to the trade brigades and the preparation of pelts for shipment. Stuart worked closely with Fort Mackinac officers and Indian Agents, who both protected and restricted the activities of the American Fur Company.

As a strategic border post, Fort Mackinac protected American citizens and enforced laws keeping Canadian fur traders from doing business in the United States. In 1816 Deputy Secretary of War George Graham made clear the government's desire to support the American Fur Company's activity at Mackinac when he ordered the post commander to "give to these gentlemen every possible facility and aid in the prosecution of their business that may be compatible with your public duties." On the other hand, fort officers also helped the United States Indian Agent on

Mackinac Island to carefully regulate the fur trade. These regulations sometimes upset Stuart, who wanted to pursue the trade with as few restrictions as possible.

While the American Fur Company dominated the fur trade, some independent fur traders continued to operate successful businesses from Mackinac Island. Magdelaine LaFramboise took control of her husband's trade outfit after he was murdered in 1806. "Madame" LaFramboise, as she was known, ran a successful outpost on the Grand River (today Ada, Michigan) and returned to Mackinac Island each summer with her furs. After competing with the American Fur Company for many years, LaFramboise joined them in 1818 and eventually sold her Grand River post in 1822. The firm of Biddle and Drew (Edward Biddle and John Drew) outfitted several trade brigades each summer from their headquarters on Mackinac Island. Biddle and Drew often competed with the mighty American Fur Company in selected outposts. When it was to their advantage, however, they purchased trade goods from the company and sold them their furs.

Michael Dousman (the Mackinac Militia spy captured and released by the British in 1812) also began his fur trading career as an independent merchant. In

William Beaumont and Family, 1832. Beaumont was post surgeon at Fort Mackinac in 1822 when Alexis St. Martin, a 19-year old French-Canadian voyageur, was accidentally shot. Beaumont nursed the young man back to health, but a permanent hole remained in St. Martin's abdomen. Beaumont took advantage of this unusual opportunity and performed experiments on St. Martin's stomach. Beaumont's studies furthered scientific understanding of the human digestive system.

1819 he purchased shares in the American Fur Company and, later, went to work for the company. The fur trade was only one part of Dousman's business empire. Between the 1820s and 1840s he owned farms, bought property, shipped and sold a wide variety of goods, and won government contracts selling beef, firewood, straw, and hay to soldiers at Fort Mackinac. Dousman also operated

An Island Famous in These Regions   **29**

RIGHT: **The Mill at Historic Mill Creek.**
OPPOSITE TOP: **Amanda Ferry's sister, Hannah White, painted this view of Mackinac Island in 1830. Despite its unusual perspective, the painting accurately portrays a number of buildings.**
OPPOSITE CENTER: **Children's toy found in the Mission House during restoration.** OPPOSITE BOTTOM: **Amanda and William Ferry.**

the region's only saw mill on the mainland at Mill Creek. Dousman became Mackinac's richest citizen through the success of his far-flung enterprises.

Despite the success of independent firms, the American Fur Company's activities dominated life on Mackinac Island. As the company's resident agent, Robert Stuart was a leading member of Mackinac Island society. With his gracious wife Elizabeth, Robert welcomed prominent visitors and entertained local dignitaries and friends in his stately Market Street home. They often hosted sumptuous dinner parties and elegant teas, small reminders of refined civilization in this otherwise coarse and untamed frontier village. The Stuarts raised eight children on Mackinac Island. Deeply concerned about their education and spiritual lives, Elizabeth enthusiastically welcomed the Reverend William and Amanda White Ferry, who opened a mission school on the island in 1823.

Spurred by a religious revival sweeping the United States in the first half of the nineteenth century, Evangelical Protestant Christians sent missionaries across the country and the world. The movement reached Mackinac Island in 1823. The great influx of traders' families made Mackinac Island fertile ground for missionary efforts. The mission teachers hoped to convert the children to Protestant Christianity and teach them the ways of "American" society. The school grew rapidly and the missionaries built the Mission House in 1825. By 1828, 79 boys and 55 girls boarded at the Mission House. The children studied history, reading, arithmetic, and geography. Boys also learned manual skills such as blacksmithing, carpentry, shoemaking, and farming. Girls learned to cook and sew and manage a household. Each day teachers encouraged the children to read the Bible and to pray. Most of the students were Métis. Their fathers were usually French Canadian and their mothers were mostly Odawa and Ojibway. About twenty students converted, but most of them retained their Roman Catholic or Native spiritual beliefs.

The Ferrys also ministered to adults living on and visiting Mackinac Island. In February, 1823, Reverend Ferry organized a Presbyterian church with nine members. A revival during the winter of 1829 saw membership in the church rise to about eighty. As a result, the congregation built Mission Church. The church roll included some of the island's most prominent people: Robert and Elizabeth Stuart, Michael and Jane Dousman, and Fort Mackinac's post surgeon Dr. Richard Satterlee and his wife Mary.

The Protestant mission prospered as did the general economic health of Mackinac Island, until Astor's declining success in the fur trade caused him to sell the American Fur Company in 1834. Several factors beyond Astor's control convinced him to get out of the fur market before it hit bottom. Import and export laws favoring foreign fur companies made it increasingly difficult for Astor to compete in the world market by the late 1820s. Furthermore, the market was changing as a result of the Industrial Revolution which made possible the manufacture of the cheap, machine-made clothing that replaced hand-made fur garments. Changing fashions also hurt the business. The rising popularity of Chinese silk was especially damaging to the hat market. Writing from Paris in 1832, Astor complained, "I very much fear Beaver will not sell well very soon unless very fine, it

appears that they make hats of silk in place of beaver." Finally, America's westward expansion disrupted the traditional Native American role as fur gatherer. As tribes ceded their land to the government and moved onto reservations, the American Fur Company lost its dependable and inexpensive work force, and labor costs increased.

Astor sold the company in 1834 to a group of investors, including Ramsey Crooks, who was elected president. Crooks immediately diversified the company and began commercial fishing operations on Lake Superior. At the same time he shifted the company's inland headquarters to LaPointe, Wisconsin. Mackinac Island, although it remained a company depot, ceased to be the main distribution center for the upper lakes trade. The American Fur Company prospered under Crooks' management, but Mackinac Island no longer attracted the great hordes of summer clerks, traders, and their families. The Protestant mission, which had been in decline for several years, closed its doors in 1837. The United States Army, aware of the island's reduced importance, sent Fort Mackinac's soldiers to Florida during the Second Seminole War the same year. The fort remained abandoned, except during the summer of 1839, until May 1840.

In the early 1840s, stiff competition, the rise of independent traders, and a national recession crippled the American Fur Company. In 1842 Crooks declared bankruptcy and began dissolving his empire to pay creditors. Mackinac Island was in a period of profound transformation. Furs continued to flow through the island for another decade or so, but the island's prominence in the trade steadily declined. Fish slowly replaced furs as the island's prime export product. Summer continued to be Mackinac's time of activity, but now it was commercial fishing and shipping that propelled life on Mackinac Island.

RIGHT: **A mid-nineteenth century view of Mackinac Island's Market Street.** BELOW: **Whitefish skeleton unearthed by archaeologists at Colonial Michilimackinac.**

Home of the Fish

COMMERCIAL FISHING replaced fur trading as Mackinac Island's primary industry in the 1830s. The transition was smooth. The region's waters teemed with a rich and seemingly endless bounty of whitefish, lake trout, pickerel, and cisco. The burgeoning populations of Chicago, Detroit, Cleveland, and Buffalo provided a ready market for the fishermen's catch. Trade routes that once carried canoes filled with furs now served as shipping lanes for a growing fleet of schooners and steamboats that connected centrally located Mackinac Island with its markets. The island's wharves, warehouses, and workforce, which so effectively served the fur trade, were easily adapted to commercial fishing.

Fish had been a staple in the diet of straits area residents for centuries. French, British, and American settlers quickly adopted the Native American appreciation for delicate whitefish, succulent lake trout, and a wide variety of other native species. Historical records and

"Our arrival [at Mackinac Island] was an event which soon collected most of the population on the little pier. They principally consist of fishermen, this part of the lake being celebrated for the splendid trout and White fish (like a salmon) taken in it, the catching of which is almost the only occupation of the inhabitants."

William Fairholme
August 9, 1840

archaeological excavations provide mountains of evidence that the people of Mackinac relied on locally caught fish for their subsistence. In the early nineteenth century, local entrepreneurs envisioned netting great profit by harvesting these fish for commercial markets. As early as the 1820s, Mackinac Island merchants shipped whitefish to markets as far away as Buffalo.

Although the American Fur Company shipped fish from Mackinac Island, it did not dominate the industry. Most fishing was managed by small independent entrepreneurs, including Michael Dousman, Biddle and Drew, William Scott, Toll and Rice, Bromilow and Bates, and James Bennett. Fishing changed the island's appearance as merchants constructed or expanded at least a dozen docks in the island harbor during the 1840s and '50s. The island served as the home port: from here merchants distributed nets, barrels, and salt to small fishing villages stretching more than 100 miles from Mackinac Island and including Hammond Bay, Drummond Island, Cross Village, Little Traverse Bay, Beaver Island, and the north shores of Lakes Huron and Michigan.

Fishermen using seine, pound, and gill nets and working out of sturdy, double-prowed Mackinaw Boats, caught hundreds of pounds of fish every year. The fishing season began in the spring and continued until ice prevented fishermen from setting their nets. Fall was the busiest time of the year as fishermen strategically ambushed fish returning to their spawning grounds. Whitefish was the most popular

OPPOSITE TOP: **Mackinac Island, 1870s. In the foreground, on the corner of Main and Astor streets, is the store of fish merchants Bromilow and Bates.** OPPOSITE BOTTOM: **The Mackinaw Boat, Flying Mist, c. 1900.** RIGHT: **Color postcard of a Mackinaw Boat in front of Marquette Park.** BELOW: **Fish net drying racks on shore near Windermere Point.**

export, usually amounting to about three-quarters of the annual trade. Trout, pickerel, and herring were also shipped, as was "fish oil," a product sent to tanneries for softening leather. In the early years most fish were salted for preservation and packed into "half-barrels" containing about 100 pounds of fish each. Island merchants traveled to the fishing grounds on a regular basis to retrieve full barrels and drop off new supplies.

Coopers provided an important service in the early years of the fishing industry. A tremendous demand for barrels kept more than thirty Mackinac Island coopers busy plying their trade in 1850. The village hummed with the sounds of hammers, draw-knives and axes as skilled coopers from Ireland, Scotland and Canada fashioned thousands of barrel staves from raw wooden planks.

Boat owners and their captains cruised the fishing grounds for island fish dealers. In 1851 several fish merchants, including Edward Biddle, Michael Dousman, and William Scott, used the schooners *Yankee*, *Kish-kon-co*, and *William Foster* to serve their fisheries. As the industry grew, individual merchants began running their own vessels. James Bennett operated the schooner *Union* for several years, and Edward Bouchard captained the *Islander* for John Bates. The coal-burning, seventy-six-foot, steam propeller *Islander* carried up to 700 half-barrels and usually provided Bates with speed and reliability in all weather.

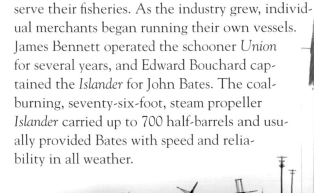

An Island Famous in These Regions   **35**

When a leaky boiler sidelined the *Islander* in July 1872, however, Bates borrowed Bennett's trusty schooner to retrieve his fish.

At Mackinac Island the fish were unloaded, inspected and repacked in fresh salt and new barrels for shipment to downlake markets. Locally elected fish inspectors carefully examined all barrels and their contents to ensure the quality

of the exports. Fish that didn't meet inspection standards (those described as "sour and rusty") were to be removed from the island within twenty-four hours. Mid-century inspectors, including Matthew Geary, William Davenport, and Felix Cadieux, branded their seal of approval on all barrels that passed inspection. Merchants then loaded their fish on large, lake-going vessels that passed through Mackinac on their way to Chicago, Milwaukee, Detroit, Cleveland, Buffalo, and other smaller cities in between. Early lake transportation was by sail, but in the early 1870s the Erie and Western Transportation Company established regular service to Mackinac Island with its 210-foot sister ships, the steamers *China*, *India*, and *Japan*, which stopped at Mackinac three times a week.

Island merchants also purchased fish from local, independent fishermen. Freshly caught fish were sometimes packed in ice and shipped in "cars," large, wooden and galvanized containers holding 500 to 1,000 pounds of ice and fish. Cars were mounted on two or four wheels so that they could be easily rolled on and off the boats. To supply their fresh fish needs, islanders harvested ice each year in late winter from the frozen Straits of Mackinac and stored the large blocks in wharf-side ice houses. Fresh fish eventually replaced the salted variety in the late nineteenth century, as refrigeration techniques and transportation methods improved. The shift to fresh fish doomed the island's barrel industry and by 1880 only Stephan and Patrick Doud made barrels on Mackinac Island.

Local fishermen created an unsightly and smelly refuse problem for the island village. Reacting to the growing piles of fish guts scattered along the island shore, the village council outlawed the dumping of "fish remains" on city streets

OPPOSITE TOP: **This view of the harbor filled with Indian canoes, sail boats and steamers reflects Mackinac's Island's active and diverse community in the mid-nineteenth century.** OPPOSITE BELOW: **Drying and repairing fishnets.** RIGHT: **Frank King and crew proudly display their catch.** BELOW: **Map of island village showing Borough Lot in purple.**

in 1848. Five years later they prohibited the "cleaning and dressing" of fish on the lakeshore within the city limits and restricted the dumping of "fish offal" to an open field beyond the western edge of town. The field was known as the "Borough Lot." Fishermen, most of whom were Native American or Métis, eventually squatted on this land (the modern-day field between the city school and Grand Hotel) creating what came to be called "Shanty Town."

As a fish processing and shipping center, Mackinac Island never enjoyed the

international reputation or significance it had as a fur trade depot. Nonetheless, the island was one of the earliest fisheries in the upper lakes: At its peak, in the middle part of the nineteenth century, it was one of the most prosperous in the region. In 1835 Mackinac Island exported 1,700 barrels of fish; ten years later the number grew to nearly 20,000 barrels. By the 1870s, however, other ports were enjoying more and more of the region's fish industry. Competition from shipping stations at Beaver Island, St. Helena Island, Cheboygan, Mackinaw City, and St. Ignace cut into the Mackinac trade. In 1872 John Bates complained that annual fish exports had dropped from 25,000 to 5,000 barrels of fish.

The business further declined on the island in the 1880s when rail service extended into St. Ignace and Mackinaw City. Markets in Detroit and Chicago could now have fresh fish from the Straits of Mackinac delivered on trains in a matter of hours, not days. Over time this effectively shifted much of the business from boats to trains and from the island to the mainland. By the 1920s only George Lasley and Frank King operated fishing boats from Mackinac Island, and they took their catch to St. Ignace for processing and shipping.

An Island Famous in These Regions   **37**

LEFT: The Indian Dormitory, restored by the Mackinac State Historic Parks and opened to the public in 1966. RIGHT: 1842 drawing showing Native American wigwams lining the island shore during treaty payment time.

The Growing Village: Mid-Century Mackinac

THE MID-NINETEENTH-CENTURY population explosion in the Midwest, fueled by large numbers of European immigrants, profoundly impacted Mackinac Island. The lure of fertile land as well as business and employment opportunities in fishing, lumbering, and mining attracted the new settlers to the Great Lakes region. Michigan's population alone grew from 175,000 in 1837 to 749,000 in 1860. Steamboats and trains (products of the Industrial Revolution) facilitated the movement of people and goods. As it had been for canoes and schooners, the Straits of Mackinac was a central shipping lane for steamboats. It was on these boats that Mackinac merchants shipped their fish. Many other supplies, materials, and raw products were also shipped from this conveniently located port. Even furs continued to flow through Mackinac as late as the 1870s. Islanders also profited by selling wood as fuel to passing ships. Much of the wood was cut on nearby Bois Blanc Island, a mid-winter task that kept many fishermen busy in the off-season. Each summer the island wharves groaned under the weight of wood (and later coal) piles waiting to be sold to incoming steamers.

This influx of humanity created an enormous demand

"Here a lively and interesting scene presented itself. This being the period when the Indians assemble at this point to receive their annuities; a large portion of the tribes are now gathered here and their lodges, hundreds in number, cover the broad beach and dot the hillsides. The streets are covered with Indians, traders etc. all busily engaged in traffic."

John Foster
Journal of a Voyage from Green Bay to Buffalo, 1845

for Native American land. In order to secure title to Michigan lands, the United States government negotiated several treaties with area Native Americans. The 1836 Treaty of Washington provided a tremendous economic boost to Mackinac Island. In this treaty the Ojibway and Odawa bands from the western third of the lower peninsula and eastern half of the upper peninsula sold 15 million acres to the federal government. In exchange for the land, Native people received money, goods, and provisions over the course of twenty years. Island merchants, led by representatives of the American Fur Company, lobbied hard to have the payments made at Mackinac Island. The prospect of nearly $30,000 in gold and silver coin being spent in their shops and stores prompted members of the island community to become actively involved in crafting and passing the treaty legislation. Their efforts succeeded.

"The people of Mackinac Island were peculiar and some of them still entitled to that distinction. There were English, Scotch, Irish, French, Indians and every conceivable intermixture of the same...The diversity and intermingling of religious views were only equalled by the diversity and intermingling of nationalities."

J.A. Van Fleet describing 1860s Mackinac Island

LEFT: **Mackinac Island harbor and village c. 1850.** BELOW: **Horse-drawn loads of firewood make their way across the ice from Bois Blanc to Mackinac Island.** OPPOSITE: **The Indian Dormitory (at top of photo) and United States Indian Agency buildings, c. 1870.**

The majority of the annual distributions to approximately 4,000 Native Americans took place on Mackinac Island in early September. Continuing the seasonal travel patterns of their ancestors, Ojibway and Odawa people paddled to Mackinac Island each summer to receive their annuities. Living in wigwams that stretched from town to Mission Point, the Native people enjoyed the waning days of summer while waiting for payment day. The treaty also provided for cash disbursements to Métis people; several Mackinac Islanders, including the Biddle and Drew families, won lump-sum payments as a result of this provision.

Other treaty provisions benefitted Mackinac Island. Along with cash payments, the Native people received goods and provisions, which were distributed at Mackinac. In 1836 the American Fur Company won the first contract to supply the goods, which included a wide variety of items, from scissors and fabrics to kettles and gun flints. The treaty also included a proviso for paying the accumulated debts of the Ojibway and Odawa. Several Mackinac Islanders submitted claims and received payments, including Samuel Abbott, whose Northern Department of the American Fur Company received $4,000.

The treaty required the government to make improvements to the Mackinac Island Indian Agency. This included repairing the blacksmith shop, adding a gunsmith, and hiring farmers to teach Odawa and Ojibway people farming. Article Seven of the treaty called for construction of a "dormitory...for Indians visiting the post." Native Americans rarely stayed in the so-called Indian Dormitory, preferring, rather, to camp in wigwams along the beach. The building served primarily as an office for agent Henry Schoolcraft, and as a payment distribution center. In all, the Treaty of Washington provided a much-needed infusion of currency into the local

economy at a time when the fur trade was waning and the fish industry just beginning.

While Native people continued their centuries-old summer journey to Mackinac, new groups of settlers found their way to the island's shore in the mid-nineteenth century. Mackinac's population, previously dominated by French Canadians and Métis, began to diversify in the 1840s. Emigrants streamed west from New England and New York through the Erie Canal, which connected the Hudson River and the Great Lakes in 1825. Others flocked from the south, including twelve African-Americans (some ex-slaves) from Kentucky and Virginia. Many were immigrants escaping northern Europe. By 1860 Mackinac Island counted English, Scottish, Canadian, Belgian, Prussian, German, and Dutch immigrants among its population. By far, the largest number of foreign-born islanders came from Ireland.

Between 1846 and 1854, more than one million Irish came to America. Motivated by crop shortages and famine, Irish immigrants looked to the rich natural resources and growing economy of the Great Lakes for a new start. Charles O'Malley of County Mayo was one of the first Irishmen to settle on Mackinac Island. Arriving in 1834, O'Malley was soon followed by numerous relatives and others from the west coast counties of Mayo and Galway. By 1850 Mackinac Island's population of 956 included 181 Irish from twenty-six different families. They were joined by ten more families over the next twenty years.

Mackinac Island's Irish population assimilated into the community at many levels, from business owners to servants. In 1852 Charles O'Malley built and operated the Island House hotel; his cousin, William O'Malley, was a successful fish merchant. Michael Early ran a large farm (which once had belonged to Michael Dousman) on the north side of the island. Cecilia Moran worked at Fort Mackinac as a servant for Lieutenant George Hartsuff and his wife, Sarah

Jane. She undoubtedly found companionship with Catherine McDonald, another Irish-born servant who worked for Post Chaplain John O'Brien and his family. Matthew Geary was a cooper, Thomas Chambers a grocer, Michael Sweeney a drayman, and Thomas Hoban and James McIntyre were sailors. Still others worked as fishermen and laborers. Irishmen took positions of leadership in the village as they were elected to several municipal offices, including sheriff, county clerk, and fish inspector. In time, the Irish intermarried with American, Indian, and other European immigrant families, creating the "intermingling of nationalities" that J.A. Van Fleet observed in the 1860s.

The steamboats which brought settlers north and carried fish south delivered a new group of summer visitors to Mackinac Island beginning in the 1830s: tourists. The island's early tourists were primarily well-to-do adventurers and intellectually curious explorers. This group included several authors: Alexis De Tocqueville (1831), Harriet Martineau (1836), Margaret Fuller (1843), William Cullen Bryant (1846), and Bayard Taylor (1855). They used their considerable

talents to describe the island's quaint fishing village, picturesque natural wonders, fascinating history, healthy environment, and diverse and interesting population. Their published accounts helped popularize Mackinac Island as a tourist destination.

To serve the new clientele, local entrepreneurs began operating tourist-related businesses. As early as the 1840s, visitors could ride on board a horse-drawn "omnibus" - the island's first carriage tour - to see the natural and historic sites. Village shops began carrying "Indian

Curiosities" supplied by the Ojibway and Odawa coming to Mackinac for the annuity payments. Though small in number, these early tourists had a healthy appetite for Native American items such as ash splint baskets, corn husk dolls, and woven cattail mats. Every summer Native people also brought thousands of mokuks (small birch bark containers) filled with maple sugar, the first of many sweets sold to tourists.

Hotels and rooming houses accommodated visitors. As early as 1836, the American Fur Company considered converting some of its buildings into a hotel. By the 1840s the Franks family was hosting guests in the former Protestant Mission House; in 1852 Charles O'Malley opened his Island House; Reuben Chapman launched the Lake View House six years later. Those who really fell in love with Mackinac even began inquiring about property for summer cottages.

William Cullen Bryant envisioned the island's success as a summer resort during his 1846 visit. He wrote:

> I spoke in one of my former letters of the manifest fate of Mackinac, which is to be a watering-place. I cannot see how it is to escape this destiny. People already begin to repair to it for health and refreshment from the southern borders of Lake Michigan...I can not but think with a kind of regret on the time which, I suppose is near at hand, when its wild and lonely woods will be intersected with highways, and filled with cottages and boarding houses.

Bryant's prediction was dead on. Mackinac would soon be celebrated for all that it offered summer vacationers and health seekers. People would come to Mackinac. They would come in large numbers, and tourism would emerge as the dominant industry. The accompanying development would forever change the island landscape. But this transformation was stalled during the Civil War. Vacations were not an option for a nation torn against itself by war.

An Island Famous in These Regions   **43**

The Civil War at Mackinac

THE TREMORS OF THE CIVIL WAR were felt across the country. Though hundreds of miles from the battle lines, Mackinac Island participated in the bloody conflict. The call to arms drew soldiers from Fort Mackinac and volunteers from the village. Many were shipped to the front line; some did not return. Even the fort itself, now an antiquated and irrelevant post, had a brief flurry of activity during the war.

Fort Mackinac had become an increasingly obsolete military station in the years before the Civil War. No longer on the fighting edge of the United States frontier, the fort contributed little to national defense as the country expanded west. Peace with Great Lakes Indians, the purchase of their lands, and the slow decline of the fur trade also diminished the strategic value of the fort. Fort Brady, constructed at Sault Ste. Marie in the 1820s, replaced the island fort as the region's border post with Canada. As a result, Fort Mackinac was reduced to the role of "strategic troop reserve" - in other words, a place to store soldiers. When the men were needed elsewhere, the army did not hesitate to remove them from Mackinac. The army abandoned the fort and sent the soldiers to support action during the Second Seminole War (1837-1840), the Mexican War (1848), and the Santee Indian uprising (1857-1858). When the Civil War ignited, it was only logical that Fort Mackinac soldiers would once again be sent into action, this time to support the Union cause.

Captain Henry Pratt and Company G, 2nd Artillery were stationed at Fort Mackinac when war was declared.

"Arrests of several prominent persons who had been engaged in the rebellion have been made. They should be sent beyond the limits of Tennessee. Where shall they be sent?"

**General Andrew Johnson
April 7, 1862**

LEFT: **A 12-pounder cannon on the lower gun platform protected the fort's south wall.** BELOW LEFT: **William G. Harding.** BELOW RIGHT: **Josephus Conn Guild.** OPPOSITE TOP: **This 1856 view of Market Street is the earliest photograph of Mackinac Island. Several of these building still stand today.** OPPOSITE BOTTOM: **Former slave, Sally "Aunt" George, was one of twelve African Americans working at the Mission House during the Civil War.**

The army ordered Pratt and his company to Washington, D.C. where they guarded the Federal capitol. Mary Pratt and her six children, including seven-year-old Edward, packed the family belongings in the Officers' Stone Quarters. Leaving the island was particularly painful for Mary, who had lived in the same stone building as a girl when her father, Captain John Clitz, commanded the fort. Clitz died while in command and was buried in the island's post cemetery. Edward was also disappointed to leave the island post, which was a great place for an adventurous seven-year-old. But he would return twenty-three years later as young army lieutenant and live with his family in the same stone quarters.

Captain Pratt, with soldiers, equipment, family, and belongings, left Mackinac as soon as the ice cleared the harbor in late April 1861. Only days before, Confederate shells had bombarded Fort Sumter, turning months of hostility into open conflict. As the troops sailed from Mackinac one man stayed behind to take care of the fort: sixty-one-year-old Ordnance Sergeant William Marshall. Marshall joined the army in 1823 and came to Fort Mackinac in 1848. The Civil War wasn't his first solo stint in the post: He served as the fort's caretaker in the summer of 1848 during the Mexican War and again in 1857-58 during the Santee uprising. While at Fort Mackinac, Marshall and his wife, Fanny, raised ten children and became active members of the island community. The "Old Sergeant" (as he was known in his later years) enjoyed the confidence of his superior officers. In 1871, post commander Captain Leslie Smith asked the army to promote Marshall to lieutenant in honor of his faithful service. The army denied the request and Marshall continued to serve as the "Old Sergeant" until he died in 1884. The fort's longest serving soldier, Marshall was buried on the island on

WALTER T. DURHAM

May 16, thirty-six years after he arrived at Fort Mackinac.

One of the most interesting chapters in Marshall's long career came during the Civil War when the fort became a temporary prison for three prominent Confederate sympathizers. In April 1862, Union General Andrew Johnson, Tennessee's military governor, arrested Washington Barrow, Josephus Conn Guild, and William G. Harding. All three men were wealthy, influential residents of Tennessee, where they actively supported the Confederacy. Johnson charged the men with "treasonous inclinations" and with refusing to pledge an oath of loyalty to the United States. Because they had no military status, the Confederates became state or "political" prisoners. Johnson simply wanted them removed from Tennessee so that they could not support the Confederacy.

Johnson sent the prisoners to Detroit, but Secretary of War Edwin Stanton indicated that they would eventually be incarcerated at Mackinac Island. The Confederates remained in Detroit while Stanton authorized an independent company of Michigan volunteers for the sole purpose of guarding the prisoners. Salmon Grover Wormer became company captain; he recruited most of the soldiers at his Masonic Hall office on Detroit's Jefferson Avenue. Wormer mustered his fifty-man unit, the "Stanton Guard," into service on May 10, 1862, and set sail for Mackinac Island with his prisoners on board the steamer *Illinois* four days later.

Sergeant Marshall provided Fort Mackinac quarters for Wormer's men, but did not have rooms ready for the prisoners. In the meantime, Wormer temporarily housed the Confederates under guard at the Mission House. In an interesting twist of irony, the prisoners were waited on by a staff of twelve African-Americans at the Mission House, including the former slave Sally George. "Aunt George," as she was known, was a fifty-one-year-old Virginia native who worked as a laundress at the hotel. After a week in the Mission House, the men were transferred up to the Officers' Wood Quarters in the fort.

The prisoners were lightly guarded and generally treated with respect and dignity. They were free to roam the fort during daylight hours and confined to quarters only at night. Additionally, Wormer gave them permission to visit the vil-

lage and stroll the island under a three-man guard for up to three hours a day. The prisoners could purchase their own food (alcohol excepted) and receive letters, books, and newspapers from Tennessee relatives and friends. At night the prisoners occasionally dined with Wormer, whom Guild described as "a gentlemen who did honor to the uniform he wore." On one Sunday, Barrow, Guild, and Harding attended chapel service, but became uncomfortable and left after being chastised by the minister. A visiting journalist commented that the men refused to return to the chapel, preferring instead to "hug the secession delusion."

Despite the many indulgences they received, the Confederate prisoners chafed at their incarceration. They missed their families, they tired of the ever-present guards, and they longed to return home. Summer on Mackinac Island was one thing, but the prospect of spending the winter there was altogether different. On August 1, 1862, Guild swore allegiance to the United States; Harding signed his oath a few days later. Both men left Mackinac Island in September. Barrow refused to sign, and the army transferred him to Johnson's Military Prison near Sandusky, Ohio. In the spring of 1863, Barrow was finally released and returned to Tennessee as part of a prisoner exchange. With the prisoners freed and little likelihood of others being sent to Mackinac, the Stanton Guard was no longer needed. The army disbanded the unit and encouraged the men to enlist in Michigan volunteer units. Captain Wormer and his men left Mackinac Island on September 30, 1862. Sergeant Marshall once again became Fort Mackinac's lone sentinel as autumn's cool winds began to sweep across the Straits of Mackinac.

Although the island's brief encounter with Civil War notoriety was over, Mackinac continued to support the Union cause by sending its young men into

OPPOSITE: **The Mission House temporarily housed three Confederate prisoners during the Civil War.** RIGHT: **Fort Mackinac and the village.** BELOW: **Sophie Graveraet mourned the loss of both her husband and son during the Civil War.**

battle. Three of Sergeant Marshall's sons, William, Thomas, and George, volunteered for service. Many islanders joined the Michigan 7th Cavalry in February and March 1864. The group included Belgium-born Gregory Lambert, fourteen-year-old Louis Metevier and Antoine Mirandette, a forty-five-year-old shoemaker. Lieutenant Garrett Graveraet, a bright and ambitious twenty-two-year-old clerk who was part Odawa, recruited other northern Michigan Native people to serve under his command in Company K, 1st Michigan Sharpshooters. His father, Henry, became a company sergeant. Company K served with distinction in the battles of the Wilderness, Spotsylvania Court House, and the first assault on Petersburg. The company suffered losses, however, and the island community mourned the death of both Graveraets, who were killed within two months of each other in 1864.

At the end of the war, soldiers regarrisoned the fort, and Mackinac Island volunteers came home to their families. Veteran Reserve Corps soldiers temporarily occupied the fort in the summers of 1865 and 1866. Permanent troops returned on August 22, 1867 and Ordnance Sergeant William Marshall proudly delivered the post to Captain John Mitchell and his 65-man infantry company. In the village, war-weary veterans returned to their fishing boats, cooper shops, and stores. Business continued as before the war, but merchants noticed an ever-increasing number of summer visitors strolling the village streets, touring the island sites, and souvenir shopping. The nascent, ante-bellum tourism industry that stalled during the war was regaining momentum. Within a few short years great hordes of tourists would arrive and change Mackinac Island into a place of resort.

An Island Famous in These Regions **49**

A Place of Resort

TOURISTS FLOCKED TO MACKINAC ISLAND in the years after the Civil War. Americans sought romantic and peaceful summer places to escape the congested, industrializing cities and forget the tragedy of war. An expanding railroad system and improved passenger steamships linked urban travelers with the country's rustic vacation spots. Mackinac Island, with its historic charm, scenic beauty, and healthy environment, was a natural summer resort. By the 1870s it was apparent that people were no longer coming to Mackinac for furs and fish. Summer fun was now the business of Mackinac.

Mackinac Island had much to offer the 1870s summer resorter. Its historic ambiance provided a refreshing break from modernizing American cities filled with machinery noise, coal smoke, and hectic schedules. The quaint village streets lined with low, cedar-barked cabins and the picturesque harbor filled with Indian canoes, three-masted schooners, and Mackinaw Boats transported nostalgic visitors to an earlier, seemingly simpler, time. Bugle calls from the towering fort parapets and evening assembly on the parade ground provided an aura of military decorum. Visitors were likewise captivated by Mackinac's natural beauty. Rising early in the morning, they tramped across the island to enjoy breathtaking views of Lake Huron's shimmering blue waters, the majestic limestone formations Sugar Loaf and Arch Rock, and balsam-scented forests carpeted with delicate wildflowers. For the health seekers, Mackinac Island offered cold, transparent waters

"Nature has done more for the island of Mackinac and its vicinity than any other spot on the shores of the Great Lakes - here health and pleasure can be enjoyed while breathing the pure air of this region. The improvement of the grounds reserved for a National Park will complete its attractions."
J. Distrunell
Island of Mackinac and Vicinity, 1875

and pure, bracing air. In the 1870s Dr. H.R. Mills, Fort Mackinac's post surgeon, declared that the island was "well stocked with life and health giving principles"-just the right prescription for invalids and hay-fever sufferers.

The post-Civil War growth of tourism was the perfect tonic for island businessmen who suffered as the fishing trade shifted to other ports. In 1872 John Bates complained that fish exports from Mackinac had dropped eighty percent in recent years and that the only "happy people" at Mackinac were those running boarding houses. Eager to tap into the tourist market, Bates began running the St. Charles Billiard Saloon on Main Street at the head of his old fishing wharf (today's Arnold Line coal dock). Another fish merchant, James Bennett, began chartering his steam yacht *North Star* for "Pleasure Excursions" to Cheboygan, Old Mackinac (today Mackinaw City), and the Les Cheneaux Islands. One-time cooper Peter Hombach turned storekeeper because barrel making had played out. James Cable transformed the American Fur Company buildings into the John Jacob Astor House hotel. The general store shelves of William Wendell, Charles Fenton, S. Highstone, and George Overall carried an ever-increasing assortment of Indian curiosities, stereoscopic views, and souvenirs for the tourist market.

Candy was also becoming a popular item for sweet-toothed vacationers, and in the 1880s the Murdick family began selling various "Confections," including fudge.

As crowds grew and Mackinac's tourist industry expanded, some feared that commercial development would ruin the island. To preserve Mackinac Island's historic and natural wonders, the federal government created Mackinac National Park in 1875. Michigan Senator Thomas W. Ferry, a Mackinac Island native and son of missionaries William and Amanda Ferry, led the effort to create the park, which encompassed about fifty percent of the island.

Mackinac National Park brought new life to the old fort. Commandants became park superintendents responsible for enforcing rules and regulations, cutting new roads and trails, and leasing property for cottage builders. To accomplish these new responsibilities, the army sent a second company of soldiers to the fort in 1876. Soldiers constructed new buildings, remodeled others, and modernized the post. No longer just a place to store soldiers, Fort Mackinac now had a role, albeit not one of grave national security. Nevertheless, a new pride of purpose emanated from the fort, something that had been missing since the decline of the island fur trade in the mid-1830s.

Soldiers relished service at Fort Mackinac during the National Park

TO M.E.T.

FORT MACKINAC, MICHIGAN, JUNE 21, 1888

'Tis late - advance is the night;
   A sentinel am I,
And beat my post left and right
   Beneath a starry sky;
From my lofty post all around
I watch and listen to every sound.

I watch the dwellings at the fort,
   And the village below;
If danger happens I report
   The alarm bugle to blow.
Above all, that spot I watch,
Where sleeps my darling in her virgin couch.

I watch each shining, twinkling star
   In the blue expanse above,
And in the solemn silence near and far,
   I pray for my Mary love:
May He who knows no sleep nor slumber
Watch over my Mary years without number

       - **Sergt. William Fenley**
       Co. "E" 23rd Infantry, U.S.A.

William Fenley and Mary Eva Toohey were married on April 29, 1889. The exchanged vows in St. Ignace and returned to live at Fort Mackinac until 1890.

period (1875-1895). The garrison was at peace, there was little fear of attack, fatigue duty was light, and social and recreational opportunities abounded. The resort community (full of young ladies working at the hotels, restaurants, and curio shops) offered plenty of diversions for off-duty soldiers: strolling on park trails, dining and dancing at the new hotels, picnics on nearby Round Island, and skating and sledding in the winter. Baseball was the recreational rage of the period and soldiers played with enthusiasm. In 1885, Lieutenant Edward Pratt, whose father and grandfather had both served at the island fort, helped organize the first Fort Mackinac baseball club in his spare time. Pratt even donated four dollars to help pay for the soldiers' bats and balls, a catcher's mask, and flannel suits complete with elastic fittings.

In the late nineteenth century the army became increasingly concerned about soldiers' welfare. As a result, officers made several improvements to Fort Mackinac during this period. A centralized water supply system, installed in 1881, provided hot and cold running water to many buildings. Four years later soldiers connected the water line to a new bathhouse, built during what post surgeon Dr. John Bailey called a "hygiene fever" - when soldiers were required to bathe at least once a week. The water system was further improved in 1889 when water closets and flush toilets were added. In the same year post commander Captain Greenleaf A. Goodale remodeled an old warehouse into the Post

OPPOSITE: **Lt. Edward B. Pratt, standing third from left, with the Fort Mackinac rifle team in the late 1880s.** RIGHT: **Fort Mackinac's post headquarters. From here the commandant ran the fort and national park.** BELOW LEFT: **Gurdon Hubbard.** BELOW RIGHT: **Gurdon Hubbard's Annex cottage "The Lilacs."**

Canteen for his men. Here soldiers played billiards, read newspapers and magazines, and enjoyed sandwiches, beer, and wine in a small dining room. Beer and wine being served to soldiers in the fort?! Goodale reckoned that if his men were going to drink (and soldiers did their fair share of drinking) they might as well do it in the controlled environment of the fort. Well known as a compassionate officer, Goodale even painted several of the fort's white buildings brown in order to reduce the glare on his men's eyes.

As superintendent of Mackinac National Park, Goodale had authority to lease property for summer cottages. In 1875 the government established two areas in the National Park for cottage construction. The cedar-lined East and West bluffs provided lofty, picturesque settings where individuals could lease property and build summer homes. It took the army nearly ten years, however, to properly survey and stake the lots so that they could be leased. In the meantime, a private developer transformed an old farm into the island's first cottage community.

Gurdon Hubbard, who first came to Mackinac as a sixteen-year-old clerk for the American Fur Company in 1818, purchased the 80-acre Ambrose Davenport farm in 1855. Hubbard, who became a wealthy businessman and a founding father of Chicago, built a small cottage called "The Lilacs" on his farm in 1870. One year later the Chicago fire destroyed much of his property and many of his businesses, leaving him financially crippled. One of Hubbard's few remaining assets was the old farm and new cottage on Mackinac Island. Because of his financial problems, and despite his increasing age and failing eyesight, Hubbard developed his Mackinac Island property into a "summer colony." He named the develop-

An Island Famous in These Regions   **55**

ment "Hubbard's Annex to the National Park" and began selling lots in 1882. Hubbard's Annex was an immediate success and within five years the community boasted sixteen modest "Carpenter Gothic" cottages. Construction in the National Park's East and West bluffs began in 1885 and they, too, enjoyed rapid development and growth.

National Park status increased the popularity of Mackinac Island, and the summer crowds grew. Transportation systems expanded their service to meet the demands of Mackinac-bound tourists. In the early 1880s the Detroit and Cleveland Steam Navigation Company launched the *City of Cleveland* and the *City of Mackinac* to serve the Lake Huron region. Within ten years the D & C Line replaced both vessels with bigger steamboats that could handle the growing crowd of passengers. Still larger was the *Manitou*, which sailed from Chicago beginning in 1893. Because of her great speed, the *Manitou* (able to reach Mackinac in less than 24 hours) carried fresh food to the island three times a week. Launched in the mid-1890s, the *North Land* and *North West* became the epitome of elegant lake travel. More than 100 feet longer than their competitors, the high-riding, white-hulled, 385-foot-long floating palaces carried up to 540 passengers each. These Northern Steamship Company vessels were the first built exclusively for passenger service, leaving the less-glamorous freight market to other lines.

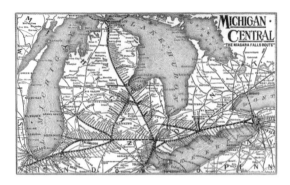

OPPOSITE: **Mackinac Island harbor, c. 1905. Passenger steam boats dwarfed the island docks when they arrived.** RIGHT: **Beginning in the 1880s, railroad connections put Mackinac Island just a few day's travel from most Midwestern cities.** BELOW: **The "Mackinac House" was rebuilt as "The New Mackinac" after it burned to the ground in 1887.**

Railroad lines competed with steamboats for the business of north-bound tourists. By 1875 rail service extended into Petoskey, where visitors bound for Mackinac would climb aboard the steamers *Music* or *Van Raalte* for the fifty-mile voyage to Mackinac Island. In the early 1880s rail companies laid tracks into St. Ignace and Mackinaw City, leaving only a short ferry boat ride to the island. While they could not provide the level of luxury that liners afforded, railroads supplied the fastest, most convenient service to the Straits of Mackinac. Harried businessmen and fast-moving excursionists left Chicago or Detroit in late afternoon, spent the evening in a sleeping car, and awoke to an early morning breakfast at the Straits of Mackinac.

Boats and trains brought more tourists than Mackinac Island could accommodate. The construction of several new hotels, including the Murray, the

Mackinac House, and the Palmer House, could not keep up with the swell of humanity arriving on Mackinac Island's shore. A truly spectacular hotel was needed to house the overflow of visitors and cement Mackinac's reputation as a luxurious summer resort. Sensing that construction of such a hotel would benefit everyone involved, the normally competitive transportation companies pooled their resources and built Grand Hotel in 1887. The construction of Grand Hotel catapulted the island into a new era - an era in which Mackinac Island reigned as the grand resort of the north.

Grand Resort of the North

GREAT WEALTH TRANSFORMED MACKINAC ISLAND in the 1880s and 1890s. What began as a modest and quaint summer place blossomed into an opulent and fashionable resort. Money made the difference. Profits from post-Civil War industrialization flowed to Mackinac Island for business investment and personal recreation. When the spending binge was over, Mackinac Island's recast landscape was dominated by a sprawling new hotel and palatial summer cottages.

It was the transportation companies - some of America's most profitable "Gilded Age" industries - which built Grand Hotel in 1887. The idea of constructing a large hotel to house the swelling crowds of summer visitors had been floating around the island for at least ten years. In 1882 Kalamazoo resident Francis Stockbridge bought a choice piece of island property on a rising bluff west of Fort Mackinac for a new hotel. Stockbridge, who had made a fortune in mining, timber, and railroads, looked for investors to share in his dream. In 1886 three transportation companies - the Michigan Central Railroad, Grand Rapids and Indiana Railroad, and Detroit and Cleveland Steamship Navigation Company - acquired Stockbridge's land and formed the Mackinac Island Hotel Company. The hotel was a perfect project for this transportation triumvirate, which could package its investments and sell tickets and rooms to the same clients. The scheme was filled with promise, and the company soon joined forces with hotel man John Oliver Plank. Plank agreed to manage the hotel, but he wanted a place of prominence. What was to be the "Grand Hotel" now became "Plank's Grand Hotel." Plank also provided a rough architectural

"Mackinaw Island is undoubtedly the most interesting and attractive of the northern resorts, and since the erection of the magnificent new hotel, " The Grand," its hotel accommodations are unexcelled."
Detroit Visitors' Gazette 1889

An Island Famous in These Regions   **59**

A Tale of Two Cities - RIGHT: View of island village in the 1870s; OPPOSITE: The village in the 1880s after several seasons of tourism success. BELOW LEFT: Charles W. Caskey, builder of Grand Hotel and several island summer cottages. BELOW RIGHT: Line drawing of "Plank's Grand Hotel." OPPOSITE BOTTOM: Grand Hotel soon after completion in 1887.

design and $60,000 worth of interior furnishings. The Detroit firm of Mason and Rice rendered Plank's concepts into architectural plans. The hotel design - exceptionally long (427 feet), very narrow, and dominated by a columned porch in the "old colonial style" - took advantage of the spectacular views over the Straits of Mackinac. The hotel company put up the money for construction - $250,000 - and they wanted to start immediately.

Eager to take advantage of the 1887 tourist season, the Mackinac Island Hotel Company looked for a contractor who could build quickly. Charles Caskey was the perfect choice. A home and cottage builder from Harbor Springs, Caskey had a reputation for rapid, quality construction. In an 1885 advertisement he boasted of having built over 1,000 cottages in the last five years! Although he had never built anything as large as Grand Hotel, he did have the lumber yards, workforce, and boats necessary to accomplish the task. Caskey was also familiar with Mackinac Island. He had built most of the early summer cottages in Hubbard's Annex and in the National Park. Caskey, too, saw the need for a large hotel on the island. In 1884 he had leased the village's Borough Lot, on which he had planned to build a $30,000 hotel. Caskey's hotel never materialized, but his experience, knowledge, and speed suited the hotel company.

Plank's Grand Hotel, Mackinac Island.

Caskey committed all of his resources to the project. He erected a saw mill in St. Ignace and began hauling material across the ice in March 1887. His steamer, the *Van Raalte*, continued to run supplies to the island as soon as winter's ice

cleared out of the straits. Using a crew of 300 men and 1,500,000 feet of lumber, Caskey completed the project in less than four months. With fresh paint barely dry and the sounds of hammers still echoing in the hallways, Plank's Grand Hotel opened in mid-July 1887.

Even before construction began, Plank was anxious to clean up the area around the hotel. He was particularly concerned about the ramshackle condition of the squatters' shacks in "Shanty Town," the small, Native American village on the eight-acre Borough Lot in front of the hotel. In January 1887, the Village of Mackinac Island issued Plank a ninety-nine-year lease to the Borough Lot, provided he reimburse the residents for their property improvements. Plank balked at this request. By August, however, the city reissued the lease to the Hotel Company which compensated the residents. At the same time John and James Hoban developed a small residential community and began selling small building lots on the old David Mitchell farm in the middle of the island. Many of the Shanty Town residents moved into this new community which, for many years, was known as "Indian Village" and eventually named "Harrisonville."

John Oliver Plank proved to be an uninspiring manager, and the hotel languished during his brief stay. Plank left the hotel after the 1889 season. His name went with him and ever since then it has simply been the "Grand Hotel." James R. Hayes took control of the "great white inn" in 1890 and, true to his nickname, "The Comet," the spirited manager infused the hotel with energy and innovation during his ten-year reign. Hayes arrived at the Grand just as the panorama of summer society discovered the place. Social columns in Detroit and Chicago newspapers took pains to list the hotel's prominent and wealthy guests

and make glowing comparisons between Mackinac Island and fashionable eastern resorts including Newport, Rhode Island and Saratoga, New York. Fabulously wealthy meatpackers, lumbermen, and railroad barons chose Mackinac Island as their summer place. Chicago's Mrs. Potter Palmer christened Mackinac Island the Mecca of society resorters when she stayed at the Grand in the 1890s. Word of her travel plans was leaked by hotel managers and picked up by society writers so that all in attendance could pay homage to this queen of Chicago society.

The island's changing character profoundly impacted the cottage communities. The new caste of summer resorters - dubbed the "smart set" by one observer - was no longer satisfied with simple, modest summer homes. Now, in

OPPOSITE: **A c. 1905 business convention in Grand Hotel's Theater.**
OPPOSITE BOTTOM: **E. P. Barnard's East Bluff cottage after being remodeled in 1892.** RIGHT: **Grand Hotel staff, c. 1910.** BELOW: **The Hannah and Hogg cottages at the top of the West Bluff.**

true Gilded-Age fashion, they constructed magnificent mansions to display their wealth and reflect the latest designs. Massive, picturesque, and opulent, the new homes (one can hardly call them "cottages") dwarfed their older neighbors as they proclaimed an era of elegance on Mackinac Island. Afraid of being left behind, several owners of the older cottages initiated fast-paced remodeling projects. E.P. Barnard no sooner finished construction of his East Bluff cottage in 1891 than he realized that his design was already passé. The following year he added a sweeping new shingle-style facade with a polygonal, three-story tower. Chicago distillers Alexander Hannah and David Hogg built small cottages next door to each other atop the West Bluff in 1887. The following year the wealthy meatpacker John Cudahy built a magnificent Queen Anne home next to Hogg. Eager to keep pace with their neighbor, Hannah and Hogg replaced their small homes with Queen Anne mansions. Several other cottages, no more than a few years old, were similarly rebuilt. By 1893 the "smart set" had so remodeled the cottage communities that the Petoskey Daily Resorter could report: "Handsome and elegant cottages are the only kind on Mackinac Island. They are the best in architecture and the richest in furnishings that wealth can command."

SUMMER HOME OF THE LATE
MICHAEL CUDAHY, MACKINAC ISLAND, MICH.

RIGHT: Michael Cudahy constructed "Stonecliffe", a magnificent Tudor Revival cottage on 150 acres of private property in middle of the island in 1901. Today "Stonecliffe" is a summer hotel and the developed property now includes condominiums, the "Woodbluff" and "Stonebrook" subdivisions and Grand Hotel's "Woods" restaurant and golf course.
BELOW: Mackinac Island c. 1905. From left to right this sweeping view shows Ste. Anne's Church, the harbor and village, Grand Hotel and East Bluff cottages.

In the mid-1890s Mackinac Island was celebrated as the "Gem of the Great Lakes." Popular, fashionable, and successful, Mackinac proudly clung to its history while forging ahead to meet the challenges of the twentieth century. It seemed as though the island's future was as solid as the centuries-old rock formations that highlighted her horizon. Then came the stunning announcement that the army was abandoning Fort Mackinac. The community recoiled in shock and disbelief. How could the government close this venerable old post? Who would care for the island's most popular historic site? What would happen to Mackinac National Park? Concerned citizens lobbied and pressured politicians to resolve the dilemma. They responded by transferring the fort and park into the protective hands of the state. Michigan's first state park was created.

Preserving the Past

MACKINAC ISLAND UNDERWENT DRAMATIC CHANGES during the 1890s and the early years of the twentieth century. The tourism industry enjoyed unprecedented success, bringing great prosperity to business owners who expanded their services to the traveling public. Turn-of-the-century inventions promised to put Mackinac Island on the cutting edge of new technology, making everything quick, comfortable, and convenient. But many worried that development and modernization might ruin the very essence of Mackinac Island: its natural and historic environment. The community responded to these challenges

by identifying and preserving the island's special character. The first order of business was saving Fort Mackinac from the wrecking ball and keeping the National Park from commercial development.

The U.S. Army abandoned dozens of small, less strategic forts in the 1890s in an effort to save money and consolidate troops. Like many other old-fashioned posts, Fort Mackinac was no longer vital to national defense. Detractors, including the *Charlotte,* (Michigan) *Tribune,* scoffed at the

"One of the most sensible acts of the present Congress was its disposal of the controversy over the national park in the straits. When the war department decided [to abandon] Fort Mackinac, it seemed as if the island was doomed to fall into the hands of speculators; but fortunately congress has passed a bill granting it to our state in trust for a park, providing that in case it should ever cease to be maintained for that purpose, it shall revert to the United States."

**The Mackinaw Witness
March 2, 1895**

fort's lack of military preparedness, calling it "as weak as an old corn crib" and predicting that a single mid-Michigan farm boy could whip a half-dozen Fort Mackinac-trained soldiers. True, the island garrison did take care of the National Park, but the army was never excited about this duty, arguing that it was a resort for the rich rather than a park for the people. At a cost of forty to fifty thousand dollars a year, Fort Mackinac became an easy target for army budget trimmers. Secretary of War Daniel Lamont withdrew the majority of troops on October 9, 1894, while Lieutenant Woodbridge Geary and a squad of eleven men stayed behind until the government decided on the final disposition of the fort and National Park.

Closing the fort was a profound shock to the local community. Nostalgic old-timers argued that the fort was still a vital Great Lakes post; hotel managers and village shop owners feared the island would be less attractive to the traveling public; winter merchants (especially the saloon-keepers) mourned the loss of the fort's bi-monthly pay days; cottagers knew that dances and teas would never be the same without the military air and elegance of fort officers. Everyone feared that the historic old fort would be desecrated, park property would be developed by land speculators, and the entire character of Mackinac destroyed. Unwilling to accept this fate, local residents lobbied politicians and army officials to preserve the park.

U.S. Senator James McMillan led the effort to transfer the fort and park to the State of Michigan. Congress approved the transfer in March of 1895 and the

state legislature created the Mackinac Island State Park Commission two months later to manage Michigan's first state park. Governor John Rich appointed five commissioners, including Thomas W. Ferry, author of the legislation creating the Mackinac National Park twenty years earlier. Although Ferry was too ill to attend the commission's first meeting, hosted by James R. Hayes and held in Grand Hotel on July 11, his fellow members unanimously elected him president. The transfer was completed on September 16, 1895, when Lieutenant Geary and his small squad of soldiers marched out of the fort for the last time.

Business expansion and technological improvements accompanied the changes taking place at the fort and in the park. New stores sprouted up everywhere and hotels expanded to serve the ever-increasing crowds of tourists. In 1893 James Hayes built Grand Hotel's Casino Room and made it Mackinac Island's dance and entertainment center. In 1895 the Island House added a massive, four-story west wing, and by 1900 they completed an equally large east wing filled with dozens of new rooms. In 1898 a group of cottagers transformed the old farm that once belonged to Michael Dousman into Wawashkamo golf course. Designed by Scottish golf course architect Alexander B. Smith, Wawashkamo's links-style fairways covered the pastures and fields where American soldiers fell during the War of 1812.

HOPE GOODWIN

Modern boats and fast-moving trains quickly shuttled visitors to the island where they discovered a community rapidly modernizing to accommodate its res-

An Island Famous in These Regions **67**

LEFT: **One of the many colored postcards produced by island photographer William H. Gardiner.** RIGHT: **Gardiner with his dog Buster.** BELOW: **Earl C. Anthony's infamous Locomobile.**

idents and attract tourists. Flush toilets, water systems, electric lights, and telephones were among the modern conveniences that improved the island as it approached the turn of the century. New roads provided smooth rides for horse-drawn sightseers and cyclists.

Not everyone greeted the tourism boom, business expansion, and technological advancements with enthusiasm. Those who preferred rustic over formal mourned the island's loss of innocence and simplicity. East Bluff cottager Alice Hamilton especially did not like Grand Hotel - she called it "that immense, hideous hotel" - which she believed brought too many tourists to Mackinac. Seeing a quieter, more peaceful time slipping away, she complained, "I don't believe I shall ever feel as if I were back on Mackinac, everything is so changed." Health seekers hoping for restful rejuvenation complained that the island's new popularity made it too crowded for comfort. Still others noted with concern the many "human sharks" who operated businesses in Mackinac's competitive market. Modern "improvements," including the coal-burning electric plant and water-pumping station, wire-laden telephone poles, and forest-destroying road construction, compromised the island's pristine environment and historic ambiance. The arrival of Mackinac Island's first automobile threatened to completely change life on the village streets.

In 1898 a sputtering car chugged down Mackinac Island's Main Street. The noisy contraption scared horses and enraged carriage tour drivers, who feared for their safety. The drivers fervently petitioned the Village Council, which banned automobiles on city streets. Ignoring the auto ban, summer cottager Earl C. Anthony brought his Locomobile to Mackinac Island in 1900. While driving in the state park, he frightened and hurt several horses and wrecked a number of carriages. In response to the accident, the Mackinac Island State Park Com-

mission outlawed automobiles in the park. Though challenged in court, the automobile ban has endured through the decades. The benefits - exhaust-free air, quaint and narrow historic streets, and picturesque carriages drawn by hard-working horses - are an indispensable part of Mackinac Island's unique character.

As an antidote to modernization, Mackinac Islanders developed a renewed interest in understanding and preserving their history. This new fascination with the past revealed a deep community concern for protecting the rich threads of history that formed the fabric of Mackinac Island's identity. Several island hotels used history as an important marketing tool. Owners of Mission House never missed an opportunity to relate the "Old, Substantial, Unique" heritage of their property, which was originally an 1820s Indian Mission. Likewise James Cable, proprietor of John Jacob Astor House, subtitled his hotel "Headquarters of the American Fur Company," even though the house had not seen a beaver pelt for nearly half a century.

Turn-of-the-century authors wrote books

ABOVE: Lady cyclists rest during a bike ride around Mackinac Island. BELOW: The Mission House maintained its own carriage and team of horses to shuttle guests to and from the village and boat docks.

HUGH MABIE

An Island Famous in These Regions   **69**

RIGHT: **The Mission Church soon after its 1895 restoration.**
BELOW: **The Mission Church today.**
OPPOSITE: **A large crowd of residents and dignitaries gathered for the 1909 unveiling of the Father Marquette statue.**

commemorating the area's bountiful history. Dr. John R. Bailey, a longtime island resident and former Fort Mackinac surgeon, published *Mackinac, Formerly Michilimackinac, History and Guidebook* in 1895. Aside from the map and a little visitor information book was a celebration of Straits of Mackinac history. Two years later summer cottager Meade C. Williams brought out *Early Mackinac, An Historical and Descriptive Sketch*. Williams, who gathered information from

numerous sources, impressed the *Detroit Free Press* with his "succinct, exact and pleasantly written account" of Mackinac history. In 1901 Lorena Page retold the island's Native American stories in *Legendary Lore of Mackinac*.

Meade Williams spearheaded the restoration of Mission Church in 1895. Constructed in 1830 for the Presbyterian congregation that had developed in conjunction with the nearby mission, the building became secular property in the 1830s and was badly in need of repair. Williams's interest in restoring the church was not so much to reclaim it as a house of worship, but to "preserve the old sanctuary as a historic relic of the island and memorial of early mission work." Restoration of the Mission Church, which continues to be an historic site today, was the first in a long line of Mackinac Island architectural preservation projects.

As steward of the fort and other island sites, the Mackinac Island State Park Commission took an active role in preserving the island's historic character beginning in the 1890s. In 1896 the Commission discussed using the Officers' Stone Quarters, which had been constructed in 1780 during the American Revolution, as a museum. The rooms of this ancient building were to be set aside for the "reception and preservation of such relics and souvenirs appertaining to and forming part of the history of Mackinac." The museum didn't materialize in the 1890s, but the idea survived: the fort's first displays were installed in the Stone Quarters in 1915.

Just a few feet from the Stone Quarters, a small plot of grass was chosen as the site of an 1898 memorial to Dr. William Beaumont. The following year the commission dedicated the old soldiers' garden in front of the fort as a park honoring Father Jacques Marquette. The area was landscaped and the park was opened in 1905. Light posts, with plaques bearing the commission's seal, were added in 1908. On September 1, 1909, the commission unveiled a $7,000 bronze statue of Father Marquette. The commission also erected plaques honoring former post commander and Civil War General Thomas Williams (1907), French explorer Jean Nicolet (1915) and Michigan territorial governor Lewis Cass (1915).

The commission continued its commitment to land preservation by purchasing additional acreage in the twentieth century. In the 1920s the commission added several hundred acres to the Mackinac Island State Park by acquiring lake shore property near Brown's Brook and Devil's Kitchen, and the old Dousman Farm, which included Wawashkamo golf course.

By 1920 the bustle of construction, development, and modernization activity had slowed and Mackinac Island settled into a comfortable pattern of life. Tourism continued to be the money maker. The businesses that lined Main Street - restaurants, gift shops, hotels, and candy stores - reflected the source of islanders' income. To cooperatively promote Mackinac as a vacation destination, business leaders formed the island's Chamber of Commerce in the mid-1920s. Frank King and George Lasley still plied the fishing trade, and late winter provided a brief flurry of activity when men harvested ice. But the seasonal nature of summer tourism dictated the flow of life on Mackinac Island.

Another "business" presented itself to entrepreneurial islanders after 1920 when prohibition outlawed the manufacture and sale of alcoholic beverages. Well-to-do resorters, who didn't like missing their evening cocktails, provided a ready market for rum runners. Thirsty cottagers and year-round residents enjoyed their share of drink as well. It seems that no one went thirsty. Cleverly concealed stills cranked out "moonshine" for local consumption and speedboat operators ran whiskey from nearby Canadian ports under cover of darkness. Larger shipments of liquor (carefully hidden in the cargo holds) often accompanied the steamboats that sailed from Detroit and Chicago.

Mackinac Island enjoyed an extended period of prosperity from the 1880s through the 1920s. The influx of great wealth and business expansion transformed the island. Much of Mackinac that is familiar to us today - the hotels, cottages, stores, shore road, historic monuments, golf courses - was developed or refashioned during this period. It was also during this period that Mackinac wrestled for the first time with the inherent tension between commercial development and resource preservation. Although the debate subsided during the economic crisis spawned by the Great Depression and World War II, it resurfaced in the 1980s when Mackinac Island's tourism/resort business enjoyed a new era of prosperity and growth that rivaled the expansion of a century earlier.

BELOW: The Grand Hotel's extensive east-end addition appears in this c. 1920 photograph.

LIBRARY OF CONGRESS.

Marquette Park and Fort Mackinac in the 1930s.

Hard Times at Mackinac

MACKINAC ISLAND'S FINANCIAL GOOD FORTUNE came to a crashing halt in 1929. As the country went into an economic tailspin, summer vacations became an unaffordable luxury. Hard times continued through World War II as gas and tire rationing kept tourist visitation low. All of Mackinac - the businesses, cottage communities, State Park, and village - suffered the effects of this prolonged crisis. But, in the late 1940s, Mackinac Island successfully emerged from these hard times as a result of community cooperation, federal support, creative planning, and promotional efforts that trumpeted Mackinac's rich history.

As tourist numbers dropped, Mackinac Island businesses began closing. Nearly half the stores on Main Street went out of business during the 1930s. Gifts shops, candy stores, restaurants, and markets - businesses that depended on the formerly generous flow of summer visitors - closed their doors. The Arnold Line's 1934 mid-summer ferry schedule offered only four boats a day to and from the island. The *Algomah*, running for the Island Transportation company, ran five times a day. The few tourists who still came to the island discovered quiet streets, shuttered windows, and empty shelves. To diminish the ghost town appearance, the Arnold Transit Company required individuals leasing their properties to put displays in the front windows of adjacent, abandoned stores.

Like other island businesses, Grand Hotel struggled during the Depression. Even at only $3 a room (plus $2 more for dinner), it was an uphill battle trying to fill the Grand every night. Owner W. Stewart Woodfill called

"Practically all of the long established stores on the Main Street succumbed to the Depression or World War II. During the Depression and war years the business aspect of the Main Street being that of many vacant store premises."

Otto W. Lang
Reminiscences, 1975

An Island Famous in These Regions   **73**

1938 "the year of the quiet" and on July 11, 1939 the hotel register listed 11 guests being served by more than 400 employees! Two years later the hotel lost

$55,000. A spirited promoter, Woodfill tried various marketing efforts to lure guests to the Grand, including a most unlikely source: the automobile. In the 1930s and 40s Woodfill conspired with General Motors to exhibit the company's latest models in the hotel's street-level salon. He circumvented the auto ban by using teams of horses to bring the cars to the Grand. Although the auto display provided media and promotional opportunities, it did little to fill guest rooms. Woodfill absorbed the losses, and through effective cost-cutting and sheer will, kept the hotel open through the period.

Tight times also impacted the State Park. After nearly doubling their lands in the 1920s, the Mackinac Island State Park Commission saw their legislative appropriation dwindle during the Depression. The park's annual budget dropped from an average of about $40,000 a year in the late 1920s to only $14,500 in 1933. Many State Park cottagers, unable to afford a second home, defaulted on their leases, further diminishing the park's treasury. Boarded-up cottages, framed by yards filled with uncut grass, began to appear along the once-stately East and

Entrance to State Park, Mackinaw City, Mich.

West Bluffs. As owners further defaulted on their lease payments, several cottages became state property and the commission assumed the additional expense of maintaining them.

The commission developed innovative measures to deal with its financial woes. Unable to afford the superintendent's salary, Commissioner Roger Andrews volunteered to cover these responsibilities during 1934-35 and 1937-

38. Andrews was an avid student of Mackinac history and publisher of the island newspaper, the *Mackinac Island News*. He organized special events, developed brochures and promoted the history and beauty of Mackinac Island in a stream of press releases. To offset the loss of state dollars, the Park Commission began charging a 25-cent parking fee at their Mackinaw City campground and a 10-cent admission fee to Fort Mackinac. Though only in effect for a few years, these fees provided a significant addition to the budget. The commission drastically reduced lease rates to encourage cottage occupancy and sold several East Bluff homes, which they had received for back taxes.

One cottage that drew the commission's attention during this period was the impressive Hugo Scherer house near Fort Mackinac. In 1944 the Park Commission, concerned about the declining condition of the Scherer cottage, asked the Legislature to purchase the house as a summer residence for the state's governor. Since 1935 the governor had spent summer months staying in the for-

mer post commander's house at Fort Mackinac. But the Scherer mansion gave the commission, led by chairman W.F. Doyle, an opportunity to curry favor with

the governor by providing him a truly spectacular Mackinac home. The Legislature supported the concept and Governor Harry F. Kelly took occupancy in time for the 1945 National Governor's Conference.

State Park Commissioners also tapped into the Federal government's New Deal programs to help maintain and improve the park. The Civilian Conservation Corps (CCC) maintained a camp on the old Dousman Farm across from Wawashkamo Golf Course during the mid-1930s. These military-run work crews cleared brush, landscaped the Military Cemetery, and erected fences. CCC men also repaired fort buildings, rebuilt Fort Holmes, and constructed the scout barracks. The Public Works Act paid for the construction of Mackinac Island's first airport, a small grass strip in the middle of the island, in 1934. Works Projects Administration (WPA) tasks included hiring out-of-work artists to carve attractive wooden signs for the island's historic buildings. The National Park Service used WPA money to hire Warren Rindge, a Grand Rapids architect, to compile a detailed historical and architectural report on Mackinac Island's historic buildings in the 1930s. This report provided valuable information for the park historians who began restoring Fort Mackinac thirty years later.

The island business community developed cooperative efforts to promote and improve the island during the Depression. They advertised in newspapers and magazines, used WPA money to create attractive promotional posters, and convinced the State Highway Department to erect 200 signs on state roads which

read, "Mackinac Island Straight Through." In this era of cooperation, the normally competitive island carriage tour drivers decided to work together. Most of the carriages were individually owned, and the aggressive solicitation of customers, sometimes carried to the gangplanks and state rooms of passenger boats, was considered a disgrace by many. Efforts to control the problem were unsuccessful until the owners formed the Carriagemen's Association in 1932. The Association regulated fares, established rules of conduct, and made visitor service a primary goal.

The City of Mackinac Island established the Park and Harbor Commission in 1941 to help stimulate business and maintain city property. The Park and Harbor Commission sold revenue bonds that were repaid with what amounted to a "head tax" charged as landing fees on all passenger boats. The Park and Harbor Commission used the bond-generated $225,000 for a variety of civic improvements including purchasing and razing old buildings, constructing a playground, building bathrooms and creating a sand beach in front of Grand Hotel. The commission planted

ABOVE: Mackinac Island's CCC Camp located on the south end of the old Early Farm. BELOW: Carriage tour drivers spent long days lined up on Main Street waiting for business during the Depression.

LEFT: Pamphlet for the 1941 history festival "Old Mackinac Lives Again." RIGHT: Group photograph of local residents dressed in historic costumes for "Old Mackinac Lives Again." OPPOSITE: WPA-funded poster advertising Mackinac Island.

lilac trees along the boardwalk, hollyhocks on the hill in front of Fort Mackinac, and cedar hedges between Mahoney Avenue and the Borough Lot. It acquired and restored the American Fur Company buildings, painted the Mission Church, and resurfaced the Arnold Line Dock. The commission promoted island tourism, even taking over the chores of the Chamber of Commerce during World War II. The work of the Park and Harbor Commission not only beautified and improved Mackinac, but also created badly needed jobs for local men and women.

During the Depression, islanders used Mackinac's rich history to lure tourists to the straits. In 1933 the Mackinac Island State Park Commission reconstructed Fort Michilimackinac's stockade walls to draw visitors to Mackinaw City. The following year the commission held a Historical Fair on Mackinac Island. The fair, largely organized by Roger Andrews, celebrated the 300th anniversary of Jean Nicolet's exploration of the upper Great Lakes. With funds from the WPA, the Park and Harbor Commission sponsored the 1941 "Old Mackinac Lives Again" festival. For three days, island business and community leaders, dressed in historic costumes, recreated Great Lakes fur trade history for this summer festival. Although not great financial successes, these historical festivals reminded islanders of the importance of preserving and celebrating their rich and unique heritage.

Local, state, and federal programs supported Mackinac Island through the lean years of the Depression and World War II. Financial necessity became the mother of inventive means. Creative solutions, including revenue-bond financing, cooperative business efforts, and promotion of Mackinac history, not only sustained the community during hard times but also provided a pattern for success when prosperity returned.

An Island Famous in These Regions

LEFT: Workers wrap a main cable near the top of Mackinac Bridge's south tower in the mid 1950s. **RIGHT:** Before the bridge opened in 1957 cars lined up from Mackinaw City to Cheboygan waiting for the auto ferries.

Post War Prosperity

AFTER WORLD WAR II, Mackinac Island once again became a popular summer resort. With economic good times people had jobs and could afford to travel. Gas and tire rationing were eliminated and the country's rapidly expanding highway system teemed with vacation-bound travelers. People were ready for a vacation and eager to splurge after years of sacrifice and restraint. Mackinac offered a perfect place to get away from it all. Not since the end of the Civil War had Mackinac Island enjoyed such a rush of visitors and surge in the tourist economy.

By the 1950s automobiles replaced trains and steamboats as the favored means of transportation to Mackinac. New highways were constructed and old ones were widened, paved, and improved as summer tourists motored to northern Michigan. Tourists hoping to cross the Straits of Mackinac to Michigan's Upper Peninsula faced interminable delays waiting to board the slow-moving auto ferries. During deer hunting season, the string of cars stretched fifteen miles from Mackinaw City to Cheboygan. Roadside residents sold sandwiches and drinks to north-bound hunters who dared not leave the line. Impatient vacationers demanded a better way to cross the straits. Construction of the Mackinac Bridge provided the solution.

The dream of building a bridge to connect Michigan's two peninsulas dated back to the late nineteenth century. In the early 1950s the right combination of travel demand, technology, and financing brought the dream to reality. The Michigan Legislature created the Mackinac

"A new record in tourist travel to Mackinac Island from Mackinaw City and St. Ignace was set July 4, breaking the old record set during the filming of "This Time For Keeps" in 1946."

**The Island News
July 15, 1948**

MACKINAC BRIDGE AUTHORITY

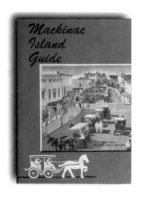

LEFT: 1954 Mackinac Island guide book. BELOW: Souvenir plate featuring the Georgian Bay Line's North American and South American.

Bridge Authority and empowered it to finance, design, and build the bridge. With $99,000,000 raised through the sale of revenue bonds, construction began in 1954. Three years later on November 1 (just in time for deer hunting season) the first car drove across the Straits of Mackinac. Construction of the bridge not only facilitated travel in the region, it also drew more tourists. As one of the world's longest suspension bridges, the Mackinac Bridge became another curiosity for straits area sightseers, many of whom also traveled to the island.

Mackinac Island ferry boat lines expanded their schedules to serve the tourist boom. In 1958 the Welch Ferry Line offered twelve round trips to the island each day from Mackinaw City. The following year the Arnold Transit Company provided thirteen mid-season trips from Mackinaw City and nineteen departures from St. Ignace. While auto travel boosted local ferry businesses it put an end to passenger train and steamboat service. The Pennsylvania Railroad, which ran the Northern Arrow into Mackinaw City, cut passenger service from daily to tri-weekly to weekends-only before completely shutting down in 1961. The huge passenger steamboats that once defined the harbor landscape also ceased operation in the 1960s. The Georgian Bay Line steamer *North American* made its final voyage to Mackinac Island in 1962 and the *South American* steamed away from the island for the last time in September 1967.

America's revitalized economy brought new life to Grand Hotel. Overnight guests returned, convention sales increased, and the Grand, so close to bankruptcy during the Depression, regained its status as queen of Michigan's resort hotels. In 1947 owner W. Stewart Woodfill felt confident enough to raise his room prices to $13- $16 a night, American plan (meals included). This was a good

Hollywood has filmed two full-length motion pictures at Mackinac Island. LEFT: Jimmy Durante and Esther Williams (INSET PHOTO) starred in the 1947 film *This Time For Keeps*. The movie featured both summer and winter scenes on the island, including several scenes at the Grand Hotel swimming pool.

Hollywood returned to Mackinac Island in 1979 for the filming of *Somewhere in Time*. BOTTOM LEFT: Christopher Plummer walking across the lawn in front of the Grand Hotel. Mackinac Island's Victorian scenery made the perfect backdrop for this story set in 1912. INSET PHOTOS: *Somewhere in Time* is the story of a man, Christopher Reeve, who goes back in time to meet the woman of his dreams, Jane Seymour.

An Island Famous in These Regions

LEFT: Postcard of Main Street in the 1950s. OPPOSITE TOP: A crowd of island tourists line up to purchase candy from May's Fudge store during World War II when sugar was rationed and candy sales were limited to a few hours per day. OPPOSITE BOTTOM: The "Fudgie Button" was one of Harry Ryba's many marketing schemes that popularized Mackinac Island fudge.

time to raise rates, especially with the 1947 release of Metro-Goldwyn-Mayer's feature film *This Time For Keeps*. Starring Jimmy Durante and Esther Williams, *This Time For Keeps* featured numerous scenes of Mackinac Island, including Ms. Williams diving and swimming in Grand Hotel's pool. Hollywood returned to Mackinac in 1979 with the filming of *Somewhere in Time*. Mackinac Island was the perfect setting for this romantic motion picture featuring Christopher Reeve and Jane Seymour. Again, Grand Hotel had an important supporting role with scenes filmed in the lobby, dining room, front porch, and tea garden.

Along with Grand Hotel, other Mackinac Island businesses flourished in the post-war years. Tourists discovered that the island's once-empty stores were now filled with a combination of old and new businesses. Visitors strolling along Main Street in the 1950s found the Murray, Chippewa, Lake View, Iroquois, and Windermere hotels. Restaurants included the Chatterbox, Astor Cafe, Palm Café, and Wandries'. Gifts and curios - from expensive collectibles to mass-produced trinkets - were available at Cooper's Perfume Shop, The Trading Post, and Shamy's Linen Shop. Outside the shops, buggies from Mackinac Island Carriage Tours, Inc. stretched along Main Street waiting to take visitors on horse-drawn sightseeing tours. Formed in 1948, Carriage Tours replaced the 1932 Carriagemen's Association in an effort to bring improved and uniform service to its customers. To promote and market the island, businessmen revitalized the Chamber of Commerce in 1954 and produced radio releases, news stories, and television advertisements.

Several candy stores were sprinkled among the other tourist-related businesses on Main Street. Sweet-toothed visitors shopped at Selma's, Murdick's, and May's candy stores. Skilled candy makers tempted visitors with a wide variety of sweets, including peanut brittle, hand-dipped chocolates, and, of course, fudge.

From its humble beginnings in Murdick's 1880s Main Street candy shop, fudge became a phenomenal Mackinac Island success story. The idea of island tourists buying sweets dates to those early travelers who purchased birch bark mokuks of maple sugar. Many late nineteenth-century stores carried "choice candies" among their wide assortment of tourist goods. But Murdick's store was the first to exclusively sell candy. The Angel and Phelps Candy Shop, located in the Chippewa Hotel, entered the candy scene in the 1920s, but did not survive the Depression and World War II years. In 1943 Harold May, Murdick's chief candy cook, purchased the business from Gould Murdick, grandson of the founder, and established May's Fudge. After the war, Selma Dufina and Jerome

MARVIN MAY

Murdick opened candy stores, but Mackinac Island did not become "fudge island" until the early 1960s when Harry Ryba added his marketing touch to this tasty treat.

Harry Ryba began his candy business in Detroit in the 1930s. Ryba learned the secret of making fudge while working with Francis Murdick, a great-grandson of the island fudge founder. After selling "Mackinac Island Fudge" at fairs and shows for years, Ryba decided to open a store on Mackinac Island in 1960. Ryba revolutionized the Mackinac Island fudge business by adding an element of showmanship to the art of candy making. Ryba moved the fudge-making process to the front window of his store so that passing crowds could watch. He installed fans to waft the sweet aroma into the streets. Over time he added new flavors, including coconut cream, pistachio, and rum black walnut to the old standbys of chocolate, vanilla, and maple. He packaged his fudge in bright pink boxes and provided small plastic knives for slicing the fudge. Ryba created the label "Fudgie" for island visitors and presented them with Ryba Fudgie Buttons to proclaim their status (and help advertise his shops!). Other island candy stores copied Ryba's innovative techniques and added a few new ideas of their own, including free samples and new candy lines. By the mid-1960s the words "fudge" and "Mackinac Island" had become forever linked. As crowds increased, so did the production of fudge, with as much as 400,000 pounds of the creamy candy being produced in a good year. Always the entrepreneur, Ryba eventually added bicycles, hotels, restau-

An Island Famous in These Regions **85**

LEFT: **Aerial view of MRA's Great Hall complex under construction during the winter of 1955-56.** BELOW: **MRA brochure promoting their Mackinac Island conferences.** OPPOSITE: **Mackinac College buildings, later remodeled into a summer resort.**

rants, and gift stores to his Mackinac Island empire.

Moral Re-Armament (MRA) became a major presence on Mackinac Island in the 1950s and '60s. Frank Buchman launched MRA in 1938 as European countries armed for war. The charismatic leader called for a program of "moral and spiritual rearmament" based on a belief in God and adherence to the four absolute standards of honesty, purity, unselfishness, and love. Buchman brought MRA to Mackinac Island in 1942 and leased the abandoned Island House hotel. In exchange for a one-dollar-per-year lease, MRA agreed to restore the old hotel. By mid-summer they had transformed the dilapidated structure into their first training and conference center. MRA lost the Island House lease in the late 1940s and was forced to find a new meeting place. After temporarily headquartering at Grand Hotel in 1949-1951, MRA purchased property at Mission Point and developed a major conference facility.

Between 1954 and 1960, MRA constructed a theater, film studio/fine arts building, residence building, and the Great Hall Complex including conference rooms, dining rooms, kitchens, and dormitory-residences. The construction and maintenance of these facilities provided much-needed employment for Mackinac Island residents, especially during the winter. With expanded facilities, MRA brought a world-wide audience to Mackinac Island. Their conferences usually focused on breaking down barriers between groups and encouraging people to work together. Much effort was expended in resolving disputes between labor and management.

MRA often used theatrical performances to communicate their message. At first it was live theater, initially

MRA
'MORAL RE-ARMAMENT'

MRA THEATER

MACKINAC ISLAND
MICHIGAN

On the Island of Mackinac stand the Moral Re-Armament Assembly Buildings, where year by year people of every nation, race and color come from every continent, for training in an idea to unite men and remake the world.

IT IS NOT WHO IS RIGHT, BUT WHAT IS RIGHT

performed on the Mackinac stage and then taken to cities around the world. "Up With People," a well-known touring group of actors, singers and dancers, began in the mid-1960s as an MRA-sponsored movement called "Sing Out." To further spread their message, MRA also produced motion pictures on Mackinac Island. In 1959-60 they constructed a huge state-of-the-art film studio which included two sound stages, orchestral rehearsal rooms, set design and construction shops, and laboratories for processing and editing film. Several motion pictures, including "The Crowning Experience," were produced at Mackinac and distributed across the globe.

In 1965, Buchman's successor, Peter Howard, conceived the idea of creating Mackinac College. Howard reasoned that a college would fill the conference buildings in the winter and provide another MRA training venue. MRA deeded the island property to Mackinac  College which opened its doors for students in 1966. For two years the student body grew and the college expanded. Then, in 1969, it became apparent that the college could not meet its financial obligations. The board of trustees committed the college to one more year of operation, thereby allowing the charter class to graduate.

When the college closed its doors, MRA's Mackinac Island chapter came to a close. MRA shifted efforts to its summer conference and training center in Caux, Switzerland, and other outreach programs. The Reverend Rex Humbard of the Cathedral of Tomorrow in Akron, Ohio purchased the island buildings in 1971 and reopened a college under the same name in September 1972. Less than a year later, Mackinac College once again closed its doors, this time for good. The complex did not remain idle for long. The island's booming tourism industry prompted investors to transform the facility into a summer hotel which eventually became Mission Point Resort.

Just as Mackinac College closed it doors, another new innovation threatened to bring dramatic change to Mackinac Island: snowmobiles. Ever since Patrick Sinclair hauled pieces of Fort Michilimackinac across the ice to build Fort Mackinac in the 1780s, islanders depended on horse, oxen, and dog teams to cross the frozen straits. The auto ban forced islanders to use these primitive means of transportation long after their mainland counterparts had switched to motorized vehicles. Air sleds (large ice-running sleds powered by airplane

LEFT: Nathan Edgecomb brought his first "rolling chair" to Mackinac Island in 1926. For over forty years Edgecomb's wicker chairs provided quick trips to town and moonlight rides along the boardwalk for Grand Hotel guests and West Bluff cottagers.

engines) first appeared in the mid-twentieth century on the "ice bridge" connecting Mackinac Island and St. Ignace. But air sleds only ran to the island's shore, where loads were transferred to horse-drawn sleighs. With the advent of snowmobiles in the 1960s, Mackinac Islanders clamored for additional access to island roads, especially those leading to the "ice bridge."

Village officials acquiesced to local demands in 1969 but the Mackinac Island State Park Commission initially rejected any change in the motor vehicle ban. Protests from the community grew. Some argued that snowmobiles would stimulate winter tourism on Mackinac Island. Others, including Mayor Otto "Bud" Emmons, argued that snowmobiles were a convenience that islanders were entitled to. In a 1970 public hearing on the subject, Mayor Emmons insisted, "You cannot stop progress - and snowmobiles are progress." Bowing to local pressure, the commission first granted permits in December 1970 on only one road that led from Harrisonville to the beach at British Landing. Over the years the number of desig-

Miles of snow-covered ice surround Mackinac Island during cold winters.

nated roads increased, but snowmobiles are still banned on the majority of park roads and trails.

The introduction of snowmobiles was just one of many twentieth-century "improvements" that threatened Mackinac Island's historic ambiance. While the community and its visitors wanted the convenience and safety of microwave towers, satellite dishes, waste-treatment plants, and high-tech ambulances and fire engines, there was also a strong desire to restore and preserve the historic wonders of Mackinac. In the 1950s the Mackinac Island State Park Commission launched its historic preservation program to protect buildings of architectural significance and share the island's fascinating history with visitors.

ABOVE: Small evergreens mark the "ice bridge" used by snowmobilers traveling between Mackinac Island and St. Ignace. LEFT: Air sleds ferried people and supplies across the ice in the 1950s and 1960s.

An Island Famous in These Regions   **89**

LEFT: The Early House, restored as the Beaumont Memorial. BELOW: An early 1960's tour guide poses at Fort Mackinac's lower gun platform. OPPOSITE: A 1994 aerial view of Fort Mackinac and the harbor.

Preserving Mackinac for Today and Tomorrow

THE PRESERVATION OF MACKINAC HISTORY was not a new concept in the 1950s. The legislation creating Mackinac National Park in 1875 called for the protection of the island's curiosities, which included its historic buildings. Local citizens got on the historic preservation bandwagon in the 1890s when they purchased and restored Mission Church, and led the fight to create a state park from the federal reserve. History became a rallying point for Depression-era islanders looking for something unique to promote to the traveling public. But it was the return of tourists after World War II that set in motion the most dramatic preservation efforts.

The post-war crowds of tourists discovered many deteriorating historic buildings on Mackinac Island. Two of these buildings, the Early and Biddle houses on Market Street, were given to the Mackinac Island State Park Commission during the war. In partnership with private benefactors, the commission opened both of these buildings to the public in the 1950s. The Michigan State Medical Society

". . . the commission will increase the beauty and utility of said state park facilities and provide recreational, historical or other facilities for the benefit and enjoyment of the public. . ."

Act 201
Public Acts of Michigan
1958

restored the Early House as the Beaumont Memorial to commemorate the life and work of Dr. William Beaumont. While Michigan doctors tended to the Beaumont Memorial, the state's architects and builders tackled the Biddle House, an eighteenth-century log home. The Michigan Society of Architects and Michigan Builders spent $75,000 to restore and furnish the Biddle House, one of Michigan's oldest private residences. In 1954 the commission also received the Mission Church as a gift from church trustees. Over the years, the commission used its own skilled staff to restore this important historic building.

Efforts to restore and open Mackinac Island's downtown historic buildings drew applause, but the real prize for historians and visitors alike was the deteriorating bluff-top fort overlooking the harbor. Restoring and interpreting Fort Mackinac would be expensive. But in 1957 the newly reordered commission, under the dynamic leadership of Grand Hotel owner W. Stewart Woodfill, pos-

sessed the imagination and desire to undertake the task successfully.

After failing to secure a $500,000 appropriation from the legislature, Woodfill decided to follow the financing example set by the Mackinac Bridge Authority and Park and Harbor Commission: revenue bonds. In 1958 the commission received legislative authority to issue bonds and use the proceeds to build, restore, and reconstruct buildings and hire professional museum consultants to install exhibits and displays. Of course revenue bonds required some source of revenue. The commission predicated all their financial plans on the hope that people would willingly pay to see the rejuvenated fort: fifty cents for adults, twenty-five cents for children. Although they could borrow up to $125,000, the commission initially sold bonds totaling only $50,000 and opened the fort with a dramatic new exhibit in the soldiers' barracks on June 15, 1958. Eager to see the improvements, 118,000 island visitors flocked to the fort in the first summer, paying more than $54,000 in admissions - enough to repay the entire debt. With sustained financial success, the commission expanded its historical programs to the

mainland and reconstructed and opened Colonial Michilimackinac (1959) and Historic Mill Creek (1984) in Mackinaw City. These programs ensure that the rich, varied, and important history of the Straits of Mackinac will be preserved and shared with straits-area visitors for decades to come.

Today Mackinac Island remains a summer gathering place, just as it was centuries ago when the first Native Americans came here to fish and worship. The seasonal pattern of life -busy in the summer, quiet in the winter - still characterizes the "land of the Great Turtle." Mackinac Island also remains a special place, "famous" in Dablon's words, but for different reasons. In fact it is the variety and combination of Mackinac's "famous" epochs - faith, furs, fish, forts, fun, and fudge - that make it so attractive. But what about the future? Who will be tomorrow's gatherers? What will draw people here in the summer? Will winter tourism change the pattern of life on Mackinac Island? How will growth and preservation be reconciled?

The preservation of Mackinac Island's natural and historic sites takes on added significance as the tourism industry continues to grow. In the last quarter of the twentieth century, Mackinac Island has enjoyed unparalleled economic success. Ironically, the by-products of success—expansion, development, modernization, new infrastructure—also threaten the source of success, Mackinac's historic charm and natural beauty. As in the 1890s, historic and natural preservation provide important checks against the overdevelopment of resources. Mackinac's ability to blend new innovations and opportunities with its scenic beauty and historic ambiance will shape its journey into the future.

For Further Reading

Andrews, Roger M.
   Old Fort Mackinac on the Hill of History, Menominee, Michigan. 1938.

Armour, David A.
   100 Years at Mackinac: A Centennial History of the Mackinac Island State Park Commission, 1895-1995. Mackinac Island State Park Commission, Mackinac Island, Michigan. 1995.

Armour, David A. and Keith R. Widder
   At the Crossroads: Michilimackinac During the American Revolution, rev. ed. Mackinac Island State Park Commission, Mackinac Island, Michigan. 1986.

   Michilimackinac: A Handbook to the Site. Mackinac Island State Park Commission, Mackinac Island, Michigan. 1990.

Bailey, John R. *Mackinac, Formerly Michilimackinac: A History and Guide Book with Maps.* 6th edition. Grand Rapids, Michigan. 1909. First published 1895.

Disturnell, J.
   Island of Mackinac. Philadelphia, Pennsylvania. 1875.

Dunnigan, Brian L.
   Fort Holmes. Mackinac Island State Park Commission, Mackinac Island, Michigan. 1984.

   King's Men at Mackinac: The British Garrisons, 1780-1796. Mackinac Island State Park Commission, Mackinac Island, Michigan. 1973.

   The British Army at Mackinac, 1812-1815. Mackinac Island State Park Commission, Mackinac Island, Michigan. 1980.

Gringhuis, Dirk
   The Lore of the Great Turtle: Indian Legends of Mackinac Retold. Mackinac Island State Park Commission, Mackinac Island, Michigan. 1970.

Haeger, John Denis
   John Jacob Astor: Business and Finance in the Early Republic. Detroit, Michigan. 1991.

Horsman, Reginald
  Frontier Doctor: William Beaumont, America's First Great Medical Scientist.
  Columbia and London. 1996

Kelton, Dwight H.
  Annals of Fort Mackinac. 1882. Reprinted with Introduction by Phil Porter.
  Mackinac Island State Park Commission, Mackinac Island, Michigan. 1992.

Lavender, David
  The Fist in the Wilderness. Garden City, New York. 1964.

May, George S.
  War 1812. Mackinac Island State Park Commission, Mackinac Island,
  Michigan. 1962.

McCabe, John
  Grand Hotel, Mackinac Island. Sault Ste. Marie, Michigan. 1987.

McKee, Russell, Editor
  Mackinac: The Gathering Place. Lansing, Michigan. 1981.

Nicholas, Edward
  The Chaplain's Lady: Life and Love at Fort Mackinac. Mackinac Island State
  Park Commission, Mackinac Island, Michigan. 1987.

Petersen, Eugene T.
  Inside Mackinac. St. Ignace, Michigan. 1990.

  Mackinac in Restoration. Mackinac Island State Park Commission, Mackinac
  Island, Michigan. 1983.

  Mackinac Island: Its History in Pictures. Mackinac Island State Park
  Commission, Mackinac Island, Michigan. 1973.

Piljac, Pamela A. And Thomas M. Piljac
  Mackinac Island: Historic Frontier, Vacation Resort, Timeless Wonderland.
  Portage, Indiana. 1988.

Porter, Phil
  *The Eagle at Mackinac: The Establishment of United States Military and Civil
  Authority on Mackinac Island, 1796-1802.* Mackinac Island State Park
  Commission, Mackinac Island, Michigan. 1991.

View From the Veranda: The History and Architecture of the Summer Cottages on Mackinac Island. Mackinac Island State Park Commission, Mackinac Island, Michigan. 1981.

The Wonder of Mackinac: A Guide to the Natural History of Mackinac Island. Mackinac Island State Park Commission, Mackinac Island, Michigan. 1984.

Ranville, Judy and Nancy Campbell
Memories of Mackinaw. Petoskey, Michigan. 1976.

Strickland, W.P.
Old Mackinac; or, The Fortress of the Lakes. Philadelphia, Pennsylvania. 1860.

Van Fleet, Rev. J.A.
Old and New Mackinac. Ann Arbor, Michigan. 1870.

Widder, Keith R.
Dr. William Beaumont: The Mackinac Years. Mackinac Island State Park Commission, Mackinac Island, Michigan. 1975.

Mackinac National Park, 1875-1895. Mackinac Island State Park Commission, Mackinac Island, Michigan. 1975.

Reveille Till Taps: Soldier Life at Fort Mackinac, 1780-1895. Mackinac Island State Park Commission, Mackinac Island, Michigan. 1972.

Williams, Meade C.
Early Mackinac: A Sketch Historical and Descriptive. 1897/1901/1912. Reprinted with an Introductory Essay by Larry Massie. Au Train, Michigan. 1987.

Wood, Edwin O.
Historic Mackinac: The Historical, Picturesque and Legendary Features of the Mackinac County. 2 Vols. New York. 1918.